VIVA
RONALDO!

THE SECOND COMING OF CRISTIANO

BY HARRY HARRIS

First published in 2021

EMPIRE PUBLICATIONS

1 Newton Street, Manchester M1 1HW

© Harry Harris 2021

ISBN: 9798486053078

CONTENTS

ABOUT THE AUTHOR

Harry Harris is a Double winner of the British Sports Journalist of the Year award and was honoured by the prestigious Variety Club of Great Britain with their Silver Heart trophy for 'Contribution to Sports Journalism' and is also a Double winner of the Sports Story of the Year award, the only journalist ever to win the accolade twice. He has earned a total of 24 industry awards.

Regular football analyst on TV news and sports programmes; Richard & Judy, Newsnight, BBC News and ITV News at Ten, Sky, Setanta. Radio 5 Live, Radio 4, and TalkSport. Interviewed on Football Focus, original guest on Hold The Back Page and Jimmy Hill's Sunday Supplement on Sky. He appears in a number of TV documentaries and profiles

Arguably the most prolific writer of best selling football books of his generation. Among more than 80 books are the highly acclaimed best seller in the UK and the States Pelé - His Life and Times, Gullit: The Chelsea Diary, All The Way Jose, Chelsea Century, Chelski plus autobiographies of Ruud Gullit, Paul Merson, Glenn Hoddle, Gary Mabbutt, Terry Neill, Bill Nicholson and biographies of Roman Abramovich, Jurgen Klinsmann, Sir Alex Ferguson, Jose Mourinho, Terry Venables, Franco Zola and Luca Vialli. Harry also co-wrote George Best's last book Hard Tackles & Dirty Baths and has commemorated Sir Alex Ferguson's 80th year with the book Sir Alex - Simply The Best.

One of the most influential football columnists for

three decades, one of the most acclaimed investigative journalists of his generation on the London Evening News, Daily Mail, Daily Mirror, Daily Express, Daily Star, Sunday Express and Star on Sunday, More recently in the Daily & Sunday Telegraph as part of an Investigative Team that investigated the death of Emiliano Sala he has also contributed to documentaries on Ossie Ardiles, Kenny Sansom, Kerry Dixon and Ron 'Chopper' Harris.

ACKNOWLEDGEMENTS

Many thanks to Nicky Butt for an enlightening and informative Foreword having been there right at the start as the man who was subbed off when Cristiano Ronaldo made his first Manchester United debut

Thanks to everyone at Empire Publications in Manchester, especially John and Ash

FOREWORD BY NICKY BUTT

Time flies. Was it really all those years ago that Cristiano Ronaldo made his first Manchester United debut, coming on as a substitute against Bolton when I was the one to come off? Of course no one is happy to be taken off but when Sir Alex made the substitution, to be fair, the game was just about won, and the manager wanted to give the new youngster a run out as soon as he could. As the change was made on the touchline I said to Cristiano, 'good luck, enjoy it'. We were all aware that it wouldn't be easy for an 18 year old coming to a new country and playing in a league where the intensity and pace is far greater than he had ever been used to in Portuguese football.

The first thing he did when Cristiano came on was to dribble at people and he immediately got the fans on their feet with his trickery. It's all about history when it comes to Manchester United, and the club's history is steeped in a brand of football harping back to the days of Sir Matt, when it was an intoxicating blend of entertaining and winning football that got the fans excited, and wanting more.

Cristiano had only just arrived at the club but what we saw as players when he came on in that game was hardly much of a surprise. Even in those few days of training we had all seen his immense talents, and in fact we had all seen it first of all when he played against us in a pre-season gamed when he was with Sporting Lisbon.

As players we were all conscious of the ideology and philosophy of the club as well as the desire to be successful.

We all appreciated that people in Manchester deserved to be entertained when they spent their hard earned money to come to watch us, and here they got an early glimpse of this new boy Cristiano Ronaldo and they loved what they could see of him.

Popular with the fans, he was also well liked in the dressing room, there was nothing to dislike about him, he was a really nice lad, he embraced everything, including the dressing room banter, which can be harsh at times, but nothing seemed to faze him. He was to emerge as a genius but it wasn't just about his talents that took him right to the top, what we could see every day in training was just how hard he worked. It is often said that certain players worked hard, stayed behind for some extra training or to practise their techniques, but with Cristiano it was total dedication, total commitment, and total hard work. I often say to my son, 'work hard', because that is what got Cristiano Ronaldo to the top of his profession. He didn't have a God given physique, or as it appeared to be God given, it wasn't given, he worked hard to achieve it. He actually came to us as a skinny, scrawny young kid, and worked hard to get that physique over many, may years. He had to reach a new level of physical strength because the Premier League demanded it, and he had plenty of opportunity to see at first hand how physical and tough it can be when he was up against, even in training, the likes of Roy Keane and Jaap Stam, and the quality of defenders he would have to contest with in training such as Gary Neville and Patrice Evra, they were all strong and powerful, and that is what he faced in training.

We would also see him work relentlessly on his free kicks, and he would tell us about something he had seen somewhere, and he wanted to perfect it, and he would work again relentlessly until he did – he'd practice and practice until he nailed it

It all went beyond dedication, he was obsessed with football. You see it all the time when some players talk about their dedication and how much extra practise they put in, but often it is little more than a pretence, maybe a touch more time practising and then rush off to do something else they are keen on, or can't wait to go home and have something to eat, but rarely do you find someone totally committed 24/7 to the game, but Cristiano was one of those. He never had a girlfriend back then, or seemed that interested in any distractions such as that, he never had a wife and kids to rush back to see or to entertain, he lived alone. He was the last to leave the building. In fact, you couldn't get him off the training pitch as he worked relentlessly on his techniques, as we all walking off he was carrying a bag of balls to work on those techniques.

We would be having lunch in the canteen or getting ready to go home and you could hear the voice of Sir Alex bellowing across the training fields at two or three o'clock in the afternoon, shouting at Cristiano that it was time to get off the pitch as "we have a game in two days – enough now!" If it wasn't Sir Alex, then it would have been one of the coaches like Steve McClaren or Carlos Queiroz bellowing at him that it was time to call it a day.

There was no need for senior players to give this young boy any advice, the club were flying, everybody enjoyed their training and the training sessions were a learning curve for any youngster breaking through. The training was so intense, so physical, that often the manager or the coaches had to stop them, so everyone could cool down!

If you asked John Terry and Frank Lampard I am sure they would tell you the same was true when Chelsea were at the top of their game and had so many top competitors in their team, all great teams have those sorts of players. In fact I would say the training sessions were harder than match days at the weekend, especially in the Premier League. Apart from the really big game against the main rivals or the latter stages of the Champions League it was tougher getting through a training session so for Cristiano to be mixing it with the likes of Keane, Giggs, Scholes and many others, it was all he needed in the way of 'advice' and he was a hugely intelligent young lad who would pick up the details of how these guys played, and that was the way to learn, rather than feeding these top quality players with too much detail, they already knew how to play the game.

Looking back now and reflecting on what he has achieved, I can only conclude that he was obsessed with football, obsessed with his desire to obtain perfection. Now he is back where it all started, and he has returned as an out and out goalscorer, so again it has been no surprise that he scored in every game from the start of his comeback to this club. When you see his stats, they are ridiculously good, laughable in fact.

There was no surprise that he opted to return to Old Trafford rather than go to say Manchester City. He showed loyalty to this club, to the club that gave him his big chance in big time football, he recognised what this club had done for him. When he did comeback it showed that he still had the club close to his heart.

When he signed there were so many so-called experts saying he no longer had the speed and was no longer the same player but even at 36 and even if he was still playing at 40 he is never going to lose that quickness of reaction, that quickness of thought. Of course you slow down with age, but if he is sprinting it is only over short distances and again he won't lose that speed, and that speed doesn't desert players unless they have not taken care of their bodies or have suffered with a series of injuries. Cristiano has kept care of his body and there has been no noticeable loss of pace and won't be if he continues to keep himself in shape. He has returned just at the right time to this club, we're crying out to regain that old successful winning formula and entertaining football. Make no mistake, he has created an incredible buzz about the place. I passed by Hotel Football, past Old Trafford, and everybody is buzzing.

Maybe it's not solely about Ronaldo's return, there are a lot of factors, it has been so depressing for so long because of covid, the fans are now back in the stadium out watching their football again but I also know there is even a buzz around the training ground now that Ronaldo is back and the fans are buzzing because he is back. It has been a long time since the club has been winning things, even longer since they were at the summit of the game winning the big prizes, but there is a feeling that those times are now not that far away.

Nicky Butt
Manchester United 1992-2004
387 appearances, 26 goals

INTRODUCTION

"I hope that I will be remembered as one of the great players, someone that worked hard, that always did his best to help his team and will be part of the history of the game."

CRISTIANO RONALDO

When Manchester United announced an agreement to re-sign Cristiano Ronaldo on August 27 before finalising the deal on transfer deadline day, paying Juventus an initial £12.85m (15m Euros) to buy him out of his contract, with a potential further £6.86m (8m Euros) in potential add-ons, Ed Woodward sanctioned a two-year deal worth £450,000-a-week for the 36 year-old.

Ronaldo's second coming created shock waves throughout world football, let along the effect it has on the Old Trafford faithful. As Gary Neville put it succinctly; the place was "buzzing". There have been jaw-dropping transfer deadline day transfers but nothing to compare to this one.

Ronaldo was even handed the iconic No 7 shirt and instantly it sparked wild sales of replica shirts – the former Old Trafford star's move from Juventus saw an instant financial benefit for United's commercial and merchandising departments with shirt sales hitting a record busting £187million. Ronaldo's was the fastest-selling shirt in Premier League history, for comparison Zlatan Ibrahimovic gained £75m in shirt sales on his arrival at Old Trafford in 2016 but that was nothing compared to this. The Premier League club, though, are entitled to only 7 per cent of that, even so £13.1m was not a bad return in a matter of a few days and to cap it all news of the signing put an extra $250m on the price of the club in 24 hours.

So from a financial viewpoint the Ronaldo signing made perfect economic sense with shirt sales helping to fund his enormous salary and transfer fee but two goals on his second debut dispelled any fears that he was only there as a marketing and money-making machine. He said he meant business, and in just one game he proved that he did. As a result expectations levels soared and a new belief that the glory days would be back returned to a club that had struggled to recapture that belief following the retirement of Sir Alex Ferguson in 2013.

In his first spell at the club Ronaldo had won three Premier League titles and a Champions League scoring an incredible 120 goals and providing 69 assists in 293 appearances with the 20-time English champions before leaving for Real Madrid in the summer of 2009 for a then world record fee of £80m.

Most outfield footballers are finished when by the age of 36, you only have to look at Ronaldo's contemporaries, few if any remain at the highest level but it is a testament to his life style and fitness regime that Cristiano has remained at peak physical condition, albeit he now operates in a different way to the swashbuckling winger cum forward who burst onto the scene under Sir Alex Ferguson.

Ronaldo had scored 101 goals and contributed 22 assists during his three seasons at Juventus, helping the Bianconeri to consecutive Serie A titles in 2018/19 and 2019/20, before finishing as Serie A's top goalscorer in his final season – all indicators that he was still capable of performing at the highest level irrespective of his age.

United pounced late on when it looked like he was heading across Manchester to City. It emerged that there had been in depth talks about him joining the Sky Blues before making his shock return to United. City skipper Fernandinho was aware of a number of conversations between the Premier League champions and the Ronaldo camp. "I think there was a chance, yes, good, considerable," he told ESPN, "I think there were even a few conversations. Also because his agent was here at the club renewing Ederson's contract, Ruben Dias' contract, seeing the situation of Bernardo Silva and Joao Cancelo as well. So obviously if you're there at the table, you can talk about everything and every possible player."

Sir Alex Ferguson was hugely instrumental in diverting Ronaldo away from the clutches of City, and convincing him to return to Old Trafford where the former boss held the conviction that the free scoring forward could have a similar impact on the current United squad, lifting the dressing room, give the players belief, especially the emerging young talent, "I think his impact will be among the young players in particular," said Sir Alex, "he'll also have a huge impact on the fans as well of course. I speak for all of supporters it's a great day for United."

In his autobiography Sir Alex named five players that 'could never be left out of a Man United side'. Scholes and Robson were certainties in midfield, but he couldn't leave out Keane either. Cantona up front, of course, but Sir Alex was torn about who to play alongside him, McClair, Hughes, Solskjaer, van Nistelrooy, Sheringham, Yorke, Cole, Rooney and van Persie but named Ryan Giggs and Cristiano Ronaldo as players he had to have in his team.

Sir Alex once told his close friend Alastair Campbell, "The thing is, I have been here while all these changes have gone on, and I've managed to adapt and help players adapt. I was here before agent power, before freedom of contract, before the really big money from TV kicked in. Part of my job is to make sure these lads keep their feet on the ground. I hammer it into them that the work ethic is what got them through the door here in the first place, and they must never lose it. I say to them, 'When you're going home to your mother, you make sure she's seeing the same person she sent to me, because if you take all this fame and money the wrong way, your mother'll be disappointed with you'."

Sir Alex loved gifted individuals but had a work ethic that dates form his harsh upbringing, and Ronaldo was the archetypal wonder player but who believed in working hard. "I hope that I will be remembered as one of the great players, someone that worked hard, that always did his best to help his team and will be part of the history of the game," Ronaldo said.

In an indication that United were now to be feared, Liverpool manager Jurgen Klopp told the press that he was "not happy" about Manchester United re-signing Ronaldo, with the club already having landed World Cup winner Raphael Varane and whizz-kid winger Jadon Sancho earlier in the window for big money. The deal to sign the five-time Ballon d'Or winner late in the transfer window had clearly spooked Liverpool's boss who was honest enough to admit to Sky Sports "Am I happy that he is at United? No, I can't say that."

While the German was taken by surprise that Ronaldo would quit Juve, he was not surprised that he ended up at United instead of City. "He was going to City and I thought 'oh, that could be fun for United' and then, obviously, United stepped in and did it. It's all fine. It's a free world and they can do what they want." When pressed to comment further about why he isn't happy about Ronaldo ending up at Old Trafford, he admitted: "Yes, unfortunately [he's too good a player]."

1: THE FIRST COMING OF RONALDO

'There have been a few players described as "the new George Best" over the years… but this is the first time it's been a compliment to me'

GEORGE BEST

Cristiano Ronaldo made his debut for Manchester United after coming on as a substitute with a dazzling display which George Best hailed as 'the most exciting debut' he had ever seen. George wore the No 7 that has been passed down to some of Manchester United's' greatest and Ronaldo soon made the No 7 his own after making his debut as an 18-year old coming off the bench to replace Nicky Butt.

George himself has been attributed with this glowing comment about one of his greatest successors to the No 7 shirt that also included David Beckham. "There have been a few players described as 'the new George Best' over the years… but this is the first time it's been a compliment to me. It was undoubtedly the most exciting debut performance I've ever seen. £12.4m seems a high price for an 18-year-old, but I think it's a snip. You are talking about a lad who, if he stays injury-free, has 15 years ahead of him in the game. He's special, I could see that immediately. In the next few months, thousands of kids will be wearing 'Ronaldo 7' shirts and asking their parents to get their hair tinted like him.'

Ronaldo went on to become a fan favourite during a six-year stint at the club during which he won the Premier League three times, the Champions League, the FA Cup, the League Cup twice and the Fifa Club World Cup, scoring 118 goals in 292 games before moving to Real Madrid for £80million and spending nine seasons in Spain before moving to Juventus in 2018.

George loved the talent of the precocious young Ronaldo, and believed he was worth every penny of what at that time lavish wages in excess of £2 million a year. I had the privilege of writing George Best's last book, entitled Hard Tackles, and Dirty Baths. Regrettably George didn't survive long enough to see the book published. The book's brief was for George to recall some of the great games, players and managers of the 60s and 70 he had played for and played against. We would sit down for hours at pre arranged meeting points, a famous pub in the Kings Road or at a famous spa out in the country away from temptation where he had been give free accommodation courtesy of the owner. However, we talked very sparingly about the games, he remembered a few snippets about players and managers, but again not an awful lot. No doubt much of it was blurred at the time, but even so to a greater extent with the passing of time. Much of our time together was spent talking about his ever increasingly complex love life!

However one subject George and I returned to regularly was the United team at that time and more specifically Ronaldo as well as the enormous wealth of players with mushrooming salaries as a consequence of the formation of the Premier League in 1992 and the gigantic cheques signed by Sky for live TV rights. Best told me that he didn't earn £2million in his entire career, let alone in a year, but he didn't begrudge a talent such as Ronaldo earning those kind of figures. As he pointed out, he was United's top earner in his time, with bonuses for the numbers of extra people he enticed to Old Trafford. His bonus was based at a starting point of the average Old Trafford attendance, then staggered upwards depending on how many extra he put on the gate, and of course, as he brought success, glamour and entertainment to the club, gates rapidly rose to capacity, making him by far the biggest earner in football of his generation.

However while he didn't mind Ronaldo earning a big salary, he had an issue with what was going on at his old club when what he described as "below average players" who he thought would be hard pressed to even get a game in United's reserve team in his day, were earning £2million a year. He named Djemba-Djemba and Kleberson who came to Old Trafford with huge reputations but were, according to Best, well below standard for United's reserves, let alone first team. Kleberson and Ronaldo actually arrived at Old Trafford at the same time and posed for photographers in their new United shirts together. Ahead of the Bolton game, there was enormous excitement and anticipation among the fans about the debut of the Brazilian World Cup winning midfielder bought from Athletico Paranaense for £5.9m and paraded before the crowd ahead of kick-off, than there was about Ronaldo who had been signed almost as an after thought.

In fact an agent once told me that he was convinced that Sir Alex was given the wrong player when United signed José Kléberson Pereira, who was born in the southern state of Paraná, rising through the youth ranks to become a first-team regular, claiming two Paraná State League titles and, more impressively, the Brazilian Série A in 2001. He burst onto the international scene during a successful 2002 World Cup campaign after impressing for

Athetico Paranaense and came to the attention of Barry Silkman, who recommended him to David Sullivan, at that time chairman of Birmingham City. Silkman told me, "I thought he was alright, skilful, but perhaps lacking the physical attributes for English football, but worth a try if he was cheap. In Brazil I was put in touch with a guy called Alex Lourez and I met him at Heathrow Airport holding up a board with his name as I assumed he wouldn't speak a word of English, or very little. Someone comes up to me and says, 'Are you Silk?' Everyone called me 'Silk' or 'Silky' and still do. 'Yes I am,' I told him, and he said I looked a bit different than he expected but as he spoke, I'm hearing a Cockney accent and perfect English. He said he was born just outside of Rio but I asked him if he was who he said he was, and he got out his passport to prove it. He explained that he had lived in Hackney from the age of about seven and had gone to study at Hackney College. He was in his 30s and when I said I'd take him to a hotel, he said he was fine as he was staying with some friends in Shoreditch.

"The next day I took him to meet David Sullivan in Birmingham and suggested that he could fix up a loan deal for the players with an option to buy at three million dollars, around £2m at that time. Alex pointed out that he wasn't sure he (Kléberson) could cope with English football so it was decided to give him a try on a loan agreement and I would be entrusted to do all the ins and outs with Alex acting in Brazil, and we hung around while all the forms and agreements were drawn up.

"A week goes by and we heard nothing, only to then discover that Alex Ferguson had had him watched and was interested in taking him to United. Back in Brazil Alex couldn't believe it, especially as United had offered close to £8m. I told him he can't play for United, he's not right for them, at best he should come to Birmingham. He ends up in Manchester where I went up there to meet him, his dad, and his young wife, and made my point that he would be better off in Birmingham but left them all to it and returned to London.

"Alex later told me he had signed for United, and that Alex Ferguson was watching him train, and the bloke who scouts for the club came over the manger and asked whether he had signed Kléberson. Alex told him that he had signed him, 'so, where is he?' When Alex pointed him out, the scout said, 'that's not him! This is what must have happened. His club Athletico Paranaense play in black and white stripes shirts, and Kléberson was wearing the No 7, but he was watching a player who had 17 on his shirt, but the one was obscured by the stripes! They had got the wrong player, and I don't think I have heard of something like that in all my years."

Kléberson was at United for two years before moving to Besiktas. In 30 games, he scored twice. Barry aided the sale to Turkey. He tells me: "Alex was back over, this time the club wanted to get rid of him as quickly as possible, their attitude was 'please get him out', which is what we did by finding him a move to Besiktas, and once again, all his family were involved in the move."

Before United signed him there had been reported interest from Barcelona and Leeds, but the player opted to stay at Paranaense because he was waiting for his girlfriend to turn 16 so he could marry her. He eventually joined United for £6.5m, first Brazilian to sign up at Old Trafford. Kléberson claims he was 'tricked' into signing for United by Ronaldinho. He said: "I was with the national team in France for the FIFA Confederations Cup. I can remember it clearly: I was with Ronaldinho and his brother/agent, Assis. Ronaldinho said, 'They want to sign both of us' and I said, 'OK, let's go, then!' I was so glad that he would be coming with me. I went back to Brazil and kept negotiating with United, but then Ronaldinho fooled me and went to play in the warm weather at Barcelona! He sent me to Manchester. That's a joke between us until today. He knows that he owes me one."

Ronaldo dedicated his return to United to Sir Alex who had become a much loved and admired father figure to him as an impressionable young man after signing from Sporting Lisbon in 2003. 'PS — Sir Alex, this one is for you…', he wrote celebrating his move from Juve with his 337million Instagram followers. Back in 2003 Fergie took a big chance on Ronaldo as, according to super-agent Pini Zahavi, it took more than a year to convince the United boss to ignore the player's delicate young age. Ronaldo was just 16 when Zahavi first spoke to Ferguson about a player the agent was convinced was going to be something extra special and following Ronaldo's breakthrough season at Sporting Lisbon in 2002-03, Zahavi even tried some of United's biggest rivals when he was initially knocked back by Fergie. Ronaldo was offered to Arsenal's Arsene Wenger and Gerard Houllier at Anfield. Wenger actually even met the player but, like Fergie, was reluctant to take a chance at such a young age.

It was only after Ronaldo rang rings around United

in a friendly in August 2003 that Fergie was urged on the flight home to sign him by Gary Neville and others who had been surprised by his performance and Zahavi was finally able to facilitate the £12.25million move to Old Trafford.

Pini Zahavi is a football agent who has been involved in some of the highest profile transfers. Few football agents were closer to Sir Alex. I caught up with the globe trotting super agent at his Tel Aviv offices when interviewing 80 of those closest to the former United boss for my book Sir Alex – Simply the Best. Prior to the interview Pini, whom I had known well for many years, asked me bluntly, "Is this for Sir Alex or against him? What will your book be about?" My response was positive, as I explained the ethos of the book was a tribute. Pini told me: "I was with Sir Alex a lot, I admired him, got to know him. Of course, sometimes he was not an easy man, but I have met a lot of managers in my time and in my life, but Sir Alex is no doubt, very special, unique." Pini was instrumental in taking Rio Ferdinand from West Ham to Leeds for £18m and then onto United for £30m in 2002. He added: "For me, the three best signings I had been involved with was to bring Sir Alex Ronaldo, Rio, and Tevez. They were certainly the three best signings from my side that I did with him and Manchester United."

Pini first mooted moves for Ronaldo and Rio when they were young boys. Pini told me, "Yes, it was not easy at the beginning with Ronaldo, because he was so young. He was just a boy, but I managed to convince Sir Alex to take him. He was the first one I brought to Sir Alex, then Rio. When Rio was at West Ham I recommended to Sir Alex to take him, but again he was so very young, and Sir

Alex didn't think he was ready. Rio went to Leeds, and there he convinced Sir Alex that he was the right player for Manchester United and he took him then. But, yes, it is true that he could have taken him earlier, but once he was playing so well at Leeds, it didn't take Sir Alex long to make up his mind to take him. Tevez! It took Sir Alex two minutes to agree to take Tevez. When I spoke with Sir Alex he told me, 'yes, bring him'. All three were top, top players for Sir Alex." Pini remains a close friend and confidante and became involved in a number of other high-profile deals. He helped to sell Jaap Stam to Lazio and played a part in Veron's transfer to United.

Nicky Butt recalls how the players had to spent three hours waiting in a car park outside the Lisbon ground for their manager Sir Alex as he attempted to tie up Ronaldo's transfer to United after a friendly in 2003. Butt and his team-mates were mesmerised with Ronaldo's performance against them during their 3–1 loss to Lisbon when the players couldn't wait to get back home after some arduous travelling before the season got underway. But Fergie and former United chief executive David Gill were still negotiating to sign Ronaldo. Speaking to Ladbrokes, Butt said: "We played a game in pre-season against Sporting Lisbon, and we'd just travelled from Chicago to Portugal. We'd got off the plane, had a bite to eat, we were all completely knackered, and we'd got onto the pitch and this young kid was just electrifying.

We were all just looking at him and thinking 'wow'. We were all making excuses after the game; 'we were tired', 'it was a rubbish game' etcetera and we ended up sat on the team coach for about three hours after the game. Everyone was getting annoyed because we just want to go, but it turns out the manager and David Gill were in the stadium pretty much signing Cristiano Ronaldo there and then."

John O'Shea recalls that friendly and the stare he got from the kid he was due to mark, "I'll always remember the look he gave me before the start of the game. It was about to kick off and he stared me right in the face as if to say, 'I'm ready for this audition'. When he performed as he did on the night, it was a done deal for everybody. From what I remember, not many of the boys were interested in playing the game after flying back from a tour in America late in the night. You're always prepared, don't get me wrong but it wouldn't have been a normal preparation like for a Premier League or Champions League game. We'd have had more rest. You could see how comfortable he was to go with either his left or right foot. He was strong in the air even at that age, and he had the confidence to try the same trick again. Some wingers might pass the ball away but he'd go back at you straightaway and enjoyed the one-on-one challenge. It's amazing how many memories have been exaggerated over time - in a good way. There's been a bit of artistic licence. I can clarify that it was the same as any half-time break, there was no oxygen tank needed for me!"

The 18-year-old Ronaldo signed for £12.25million, but according to Italian agent Alessandro Moggi Fergie got Ronaldo just in time as his current agent Jorge Mendes was trying to move him onto Italy but Parma and Lazio turned him down, although Juventus were interested and flew to Portugal to try and beat United to the deal. Moggi said: "Once Juventus declared their interest in Ronaldo, they rushed to Lisbon to close a deal." However Ronaldo went on to have five glowing years at the United, scoring 84, providing 34 assists in 196 games, along with winning a

Premier League title and Champions League.

Cristiano and Sir Alex enjoyed a very close relationship during the six years he was at United. Early on in Ronaldo's career the young Portuguese experienced the infamous 'hair-dryer treatment', and one particular exchange left him in tears, according to a book written by Guillem Balague about Ronaldo, however, generally, the word from the United dressing room was that the Portuguese teenager was given much more leeway than the majority of players when it came to the way he was handled by Sir Alex.

Balague's account of the incident claims that after one defeat Ferguson was incandescent, "In the dressing room, Ferguson could not contain himself: 'Who do you think you are? Trying to play by yourself? You'll never be a player if you do this!' Ronaldo began to cry. The other players left him be. "He needed to learn," said [Rio] Ferdinand, "that was a message from the team, not just from Ferguson: everyone thought he needed to learn."

Ronaldo, though, has never spoken about Sir Alex in anything other than glowing terms, and holds Ferguson in the highest regard. In 2015 Ronaldo got emotional recalling the time the United boss gave him time off to be with his ill father, in an episode much repeated since Ronaldo talked about on the Jonathan Ross chat show. "In terms of personal stuff I just have to say, 'Thank you for what you did for me.' Especially, I remember, the thing that is in my memory, the time my father was sick in hospital and we were in a tough moment in the season. We had important games in the Champions League and league, and I said 'coach, I need to go and see my daddy' and I was a key player, a very important player and he said 'Listen your family is the most important thing you have in your life. If you want to go three days, four days, five days, you can go.' This moment is what I keep with me, because it was the most important moment of my life. He shared it with me and this is why I respect him. And for me he is the best coach I ever had. It was a family with him in Manchester United… He made me feel like 'Cristiano, this is your house.'"

Fergie was hugely protective of Ronaldo in those formative years, and it wouldn't take much to fall foul of the United boss if anyone dare take issue with Ronaldo. Sky Sports' long serving after match interviewer Geoff Shreeves is writing his own book the same year as Sir Alex turns 80, and, hardly surprising, he tells me that he will be dedicating an entire chapter on their numerous encounters. Geoff was on the receiving end of the infamous Fergie hairdryer on more than one occasion. In my task of interviewing 80 people to commemorate Fergie's 80th year Geoff told me: "He always tried to do thinks the right way, and the right style. He was one of the best. I've been on the touchline for 30 years and I can tell you I've interviewed a few in my time, but he is the best interviewee I've ever had to this very day; he always gave you something. He would prefer to be challenged, but only in a respectful way. He didn't want you to go looking for a cheap headline, nothing irritated him more. All the time, though, he spoke with enormous passion. And if he was not happy with you, he would let you know…"

Sir Alex was infuriated with Geoff's line of questioning after United beat Middlesbrough in the FA Cup quarter-finals in March 2007. A tight game was goalless when Ronaldo tumbled inside the area despite Mark Schwarzer failing to make contact and a penalty was awarded which the Portuguese himself converted. In an post-match interview Geoff Shreeves suggested that Ronaldo 'went down easily' and Ferguson was quick to scold the Sky reporter telling him to 'f★★★ off' after being asked about it. Geoff experienced many heated moments, no stranger to experiencing Fergie's darker side, but by far the worst came after that Old Trafford cup tie with Ronaldo widely criticised for 'winning' the vital spot-kick. It threatened to get out of hand in the tunnel when Fergie came after him physically before people jumped in.

Fergie fired back, but Shreeves replied: 'Don't talk to me like that. If you want to behave civilly, fine.'

Here is the interview that left Fergie fuming over Ronaldo

Shreeves asks Ronaldo multiple questions about THAT penalty incident…..

"Cristiano, only one place to start, was it a penalty? As soon as he touched you, did you know it was a penalty? Did you feel the contact?"

"I'm not saying you should but could you have stayed on your feet?"

"Once again, as you say, it's Cristiano Ronaldo and it's controversy once again. Why is it always the case with you?

"When you hear accusations that you cheated, how do you feel?"

So there were five questions about the penalty incident, but the then 22-year-old handled it with a wry smile and without any show of dissent, and actually gave an answer to one of Shreeves' accusations. When asked "Why is it always the case with you?" Ronaldo replied with: "Maybe someone doesn't like me because I'm too good." Well, he was right, he was too good for the Premier League. Geoff later patched up his differences with Fergie and accepts he might have actually been in the wrong. "Fergie was in the right and I was in the wrong and I addressed that with him. We sorted it out very amicably, very quickly and it was never mentioned again. I have fond memories of numerous occasions involving Sir Alex. Yes, some of those include my run-ins with him, and I am sure when you Google them, as I am sure you have done, there will be plenty of detail. But what you won't find on Google is that he has been a guest at my charity events, he has been a good friend, and that I have nothing but admiration, respect and fondness for him.'

Colin Calderwood was also one of the 80 I interviews for the book "sir Alex – Simply The Best", and he told that after leaving Tottenham he sent a letter to United asking whether he could pop in on Sir Alex and observe training. He got a phone call back from Sir Alex's PA inviting him there, and I was told to "get there early'. When he arrived he was told to make my way upstairs as, "The Boss knows you are coming'. Sir Alex was working with an analyst ahead of a vital Champions League tie the next day, so Colin sat in the canteen, along with their goalkeeping coach Tony Coton and assistant Mike Phelan, who told me, "the Boss knows you are coming'. Colin was taken into his office for a chat and Sir Alex showed him the report on the opposition and told him, 'hang on while I get my boots', as he took him to watch training, introducing me to everyone along the way from the laundry lady to the kit man, and after observing training ahead of the big game, he showed him around the gym, and the first team dressing rooms were they were all changing. Colin told me: "A couple of them I had actually played against in my tine, Rio, Neville and Scholes, they all said hello, Ronaldo was there, who had no idea who I was, but I was with the Boss and that meant respect for whoever he brought in. He then took me to the canteen for lunch, and said, "you're Scottish so you will want soup". He went and got soup, then asked what I would like for main course, "Fish?". He cleared away my soup bowl and went off and brought back fish and vegetables, and cleared that away when I'd finished. He said "sorry, I've got to go back to Old Trafford to see the press before our Champions League game, I'll tell the guys here to look after you, and you can watch the schoolboys." Colin couldn't believe Fergie had cleared away his dinner plates for him.

Sir Alex was a Jekyll and Hyde, his mood swings were legendary – the smiling, approachable, warm and caring persona could turn to torrents of abuse within seconds if he saw anything he disagreed with. The two faces of Fergie are illustrated perfectly in his dealing with two Portuguese wingers Ronaldo and Nani. Nani relished his dream move to United but not the nightmare of working under a manager who was "very scary" – he was petrified of doing something wrong. "I was scared of him until I learned to understand and was able to express myself. My English has never been perfect but at that time it was worse than now and when he found I could speak more with him, he started coming to me and giving me more attention and from then, I learned more about Sir Alex Ferguson. What he wanted to do, who he was and the relationship started to be better. He's a man who knows how to manage all characters, all different ages, all different personalities. My personality in that time, I was young, and not easy. I know that and I learned a lot, I changed a lot."

Nani drove Ferguson home after a 2-2 draw at Fulham, having come off the bench and missed a penalty, one which he took instead of Giggs. "He was my neighbour and when we used to go to London by train his wife or his family used to leave him in the train station so on the way back he has no driver to take him. He was looking for someone who lives close to him to give him a ride. I said, 'OK boss, I'll take you home!' One day I took him after a game against Fulham away and I was on the bench. I drove him back home and he didn't talk to me in the car! In the dressing room he killed me! He said: 'Nani, who do you think you are? Who gave you permission to take the penalty?'" Nani said. Then he killed Ryan Giggs… 'Ryan, why did you let him take the penalty?' Ryan said, 'He grabbed the ball and I let him.' Oh my God, that day was incredible. I took him home and I feel very uncomfortable driving. When we got back hours later I say, 'Boss, I can take you home'. I drove him back home and he still didn't talk to me in the car! I was playing unbelievable with a lot of confidence. We won a penalty and it was Ryan Giggs who took the penalties. I felt confident. Giggs didn't say anything so I took the penalty and missed!"

Fergie didn't bent to suit anyone, "I have seen success change people overnight and it is not nice. Big-time Charlies, arrogance. They have no time for their roots. I see that in a lot of people. That, to me, is the unacceptable face of football. I have a ruthless streak, and I don't like myself for it. It's always there, and has been since I started management at Aberdeen. I'll do anything for my players. If they were to wake me at 5 in the morning and ask for a lift somewhere, I'd pick them up. But, then, don't ask me to be loyal when I have to pick my team. The loyalty I have then is to the club. Winning means keeping your job, and it can be a delicate situation. But I tell myself I'm not going to fail in this game. It means making unpopular decisions, but I don't want the chairman coming up to me and saying it's time to call it a day."

Ryan Giggs, who played under Sir Alex for 23 years, observed, "He was the master of psychology, he was a master at getting the best out of certain individuals like whether to put an arm around, or whether to give them a rocket at half-time or at the end of the game or leave them out knowing that the player would react in a positive way." According to the Welsh winger the only players to avoid the hairdryer treatment were Eric Cantona, Roy Keane, Bryan Robson and Cristiano Ronaldo, "They did the stuff on the pitch, so he never felt he had to," Giggs explained.

It is easy to view Ronaldo's first spell at United as one of unparalleled success but a lot of supporters felt the young Portuguese was wasting his talent during his first couple of seasons with too many step-overs and party tricks which Premier League defenders soon learned to ignore before taking the ball off him. These tricks slowed down the flow of the team as United finished distant runners-up to Arsenal's Invincibles in 2003-04 and Jose Mourinho's Chelsea in the two seasons after that. Then there was the incident during the 2006 World Cup when Ronaldo appeared to get his United team-mate Wayne Rooney sent off and the tabloids bayed for his blood.

So the scene was set for United's opening game of the 2006-07 season against Fulham with the press suggesting (perhaps hoping) that Ronaldo and Rooney wouldn't pass to one another. In the event the pair, together with newly installed first choice striker Louis Saha, tore the Cottagers apart with both Wayne and Cristiano netting as United cruised into a 4-0 lead within 20 minutes. It was a pattern that would continue for the rest of the season as United's won 14 of their first 17 games and comfortably wrestled the title from Chelsea with both Rooney and Ronaldo netting 23 goals as the club narrowly missed out on the League and Cup double. The following season Ronaldo took his game to another level, scoring his 42nd league goal of the campaign in the European Cup final in Moscow as United overcame Chelsea on penalties to lift the trophy.

Remembering Ronaldo's impact that season, Rio Ferdinand says, "I felt that as a defender, as long as we kept a clean sheet, we would always have a chance because at some point in the game, he would get an opportunity and he scores. We always felt like that, we just had pure confidence. They've got the opportunity to do that this season with Ronaldo, with Greenwood, with Rashford, with Cavani, with Sancho, with Fernandes, with Pogba. I'm reeling off a ridiculous amount of names. But behind that, the other players have to do their job."

Speaking in his column in The Daily Mail, Peter Crouch recalls, "All those years ago, during his first spell, Rio Ferdinand and Wayne Rooney used to tell me that Ronaldo promised he would end up as the best player in the world and United's players would laugh at him. Showing that sort of confidence at such a young age, before he had achieved anything, was outrageous. Then to go and do it, following through on your words, is an amazing achievement. Rio then became one of the individuals lobbying him to make that return to Old Trafford. When he signed from Juventus, I had a bet with a United fan that Mohamed Salah would score more goals this year. Having watched his 'second debut' against Newcastle, I'm slightly concerned that my wallet might be in danger."

Having managed just 27 goals in his first 137 appearances in his final three seasons under Sir Alex Ronaldo developed into one of the best in the world, scoring 91 times in his next 154 games, winning the first of his five Ballon d'Or awards in 2008 - a campaign where he also lifted the Champions League trophy. Ronaldo went on to sign for Real Madrid for what was a world record fee of £80m and went on to establish himself as one of the greatest players of all time scoring an astonishing 450 goals in 438 games in nine seasons in Spain winning the European Cup four times and La Liga twice as well as three more World Club Cups but there's little doubt that while the Madrileños enjoyed the best of Ronaldo, he was made in Manchester.

2: A DEBUT TO REMEMBER

"It was a marvellous debut, I thought the pace was too slow in the first half and I knew Cristiano would add penetration. We have to be careful with the boy. You must remember he is only 18. We are going to have to gauge when we use him."

SIR ALEX FERGUSON

TRANSFERS SUMMER 2003

IN

Cristiano Ronaldo (Sporting Lisbon, £12.4m)
David Bellion (Sunderland, £2m)
Eric Djemba-Djemba (Nantes, £3.5m)
Tim Howard (Metrostars, £2.3m)
Kléberson (Athletico Paranaense, £5.9m)

OUT

David Beckham (Real Madrid, £17.25m)
Juan Sebastian Veron (Chelsea, £15m)

The first Ronaldo debut: August 16, 2003., the opening day of the 2003/04 Premiership season and reigning champions United were reigning champions having edged out Arsenal the previous season and began their defence with a fixture against Bolton Wanderers. United reigned supreme in English football during this era of dominance having won the title for the fourth time in five seasons but one of Sir Alex's great strengths was recognising when one great United team had run its course and another needed to built. That summer David Beckham had departed for Real Madrid while Juan Sebastian Veron had not fulfilled his world class status and was sold off to Chelsea. Among the players Fergie brought in was the costliest teenager ever in world football – Cristiano Ronaldo.

Bolton manager Sam Allardyce had turned Bolton into an effective force in the top flight and he was not about to be intimidated by facing United. The Trotters had already been successful on their last two trips to Old Trafford and had taken four points off them the season previous. Ryan Giggs put United ahead in the first-half but Bolton always carried a threat and the game was still very much in the balance when Sir Alex had seen enough and brought off Nicky Butt in the 61st minute to send on the raw, yet exciting, attacking talent of their new No 7, the prestigious number associated with some true greats in a United shirt from George Best, Steve Coppell and Eric Cantona to the most recent wearer of the shirt David Beckham himself. 67,647 fans witnessed the whirlwind of Ronaldo's debut just three days after he'd signed from Sporting Lisbon, as the kid with blonde streaks in his hair replaced Butt and the crowd got their first glimpse of the boy with magic in his feet.

Nicky Hunt was the Wanderers right-back that afternoon who witnessed all the tricks and flicks from up close and could hardly believe what he saw with a winger wanting to run at defenders and get in crosses, it made life difficult in the extreme to defend against, and it was something of a new experience. However it wasn't as if the Bolton players hadn't been warned - Ronaldo's former team-mate in Lisbon, Brazilian striker Mario Jardel, had moved to the Reebok in the same summer and told his team-mates all about Cristiano. "Jardel tells me he (Ronaldo) is an unbelievable, fantastic footballer," Allardyce announced in a pre-match press conference, "who knows how long it will take to get him ready for the Premiership or if he'll be involved tomorrow." So, the reality was that Bolton didn't even think he would be playing so soon after arriving as Big Sam was sure Sir Alex would want the teenager to find his feet and get to know his new team-mates for a few weeks in training before unleashing him into the first team. How wrong can you be?

Fair enough Sir Alex didn't start Ronaldo, but put him on the bench, where Bolton's contingent must have thought he would stay for the experience but his introduction just after the hour mark didn't start brilliantly as Hunt slid in and won the ball on the halfway line after Ronaldo's first touch, but that gave the Bolton full-back false hope as it proved to be more difficult to get the ball off Ronaldo from then on. "No one really knew anything about him did they?" Hunt told the Manchester Evening News, "he signed as a young kid from Sporting Lisbon and we certainly didn't know anything about him. We just knew that he could be starting his first game and if he did then it would be on my side so I was looking forward to the game, I love playing football, and instead of him I had Giggs on my side for 60 minutes and Ronaldo for 30. I don't think it could have got any worse for me that day!"

The next time Ronaldo got on the ball he rolled it under his feet to turn and embarrass Hunt. Next, Ronaldo finally got the ball on the left flank with space to perform what was to become his trademark step-overs. The Old Trafford crowd were now won over and relishing it all, while Hunt was as much a spectator as anyone in the stands, he couldn't get near him as Ronaldo's confidence rocketed. Inevitably Ronaldo was brought down inside the penalty box. It wouldn't be the last time that happened, by a long long way. Hunt had actually managed to get a foot on the ball but Nolan pulled Ronaldo down. Roy Keane was visibly congratulating Ronaldo, but he wouldn't have been too pleased as Ruud van Nistelrooy missed from the spot.

Ronaldo was involved in the second goal on 74 minutes, turning Hunt inside out with step-overs before his cross reached Paul Scholes on the opposite flank, who set up Van Nistelrooy whose shot was saved, the ball rebounding to Giggs who tapped home. After just 13 minutes on the pitch Ronaldo's new team-mates were constantly looking for him on the flank at every opportunity. Three minutes later Scholes hit the third. Ronaldo switched sides, which was a relief for Hunt but not for his fellow full back Ricardo Gardner! Ronaldo was just as dangerous on the other flank as he whipped in a tantalising cross from which Van Nistelrooy should have scored before the Dutchman eventually made it four in the final minutes after Gardner's bad challenge on Ronaldo earned him a card, no doubt frustrated when Ronaldo had earlier embarked on a long run with the ball glued to his feet that had the crowd giving the new kid on the block a standing ovation.

Afterwards Fergie described Ronaldo at their 'new hero'. "It was a marvellous debut, I thought the pace was too slow in the first half and I knew Cristiano would add penetration. We have to be careful with the boy. You must remember he is only 18. We are going to have to gauge when we use him."

Reflecting further in his autobiography, Sir Alex added: "The Bolton defenders ended up in knots. The right-back rattled him straight away in the centre of the park and took the ball off him but Cristiano got straight back up and demanded another pass. 'He's got balls, anyway'," I thought, "he had the biggest impact on Manchester United fans of a player since Eric Cantona."

Recalling the debut, Sam Allardyce told Sky Sports News, "I'd had a cup of tea with Sir Alex before the game in his office and he said, 'this lad, he's good'. Of course, we saw him come on as a sub. I think we were losing at the time and he was playing against a young full back called Nicky Hunt. I felt sorry for Nicky when he came off. Ronaldo came on and just dazzled. I said to Sir Alex, 'you look like you've got a real player there for Manchester United'. Big Sam saw similarities with Ryan Giggs when he first started at Old Trafford, as he added: "He can go inside, outside, uses both feet and runs at people. Everyone holds their breath when he gets the ball."

George Best described it as "undoubtedly the most exciting debut performance I've ever seen. A few of my old team-mates were at the game and they compared him to me. There have been players who have some similarities, but this lad's got more than anyone else, especially as he is genuinely two-footed. He can play on either wing, beat players with ease and put in dangerous crosses with his left or right peg. When was the last time you saw that? With Ronaldo and Giggsy on the pitch at the same time, opposition defenders will be petrified!"

Ronaldo's debut had a lasting impression on his team-mates, with ex-goalkeeper Edwin van der Sar saying: "I think Ruud was used to David crossing the ball every time he had it. David didn't have pace to dribble and beat opponents, so he had to do something else. Ronnie had the pace and the tricks."

Roy Keane, though, wasn't quite as impressed. He said: "It was 20 minutes, that's all it was. I think he won a penalty, but so what?" Typical Keane. However, he had went on to put the record straight in his autobiography, "We were playing Sporting Lisbon pre-season to celebrate the opening of their new stadium, and I saw how good Ronaldo was that day. He was playing for Sporting and he was up against John O'Shea. Sheasy ended up seeing the club doctor at half-time because he was having dizzy spells; he was being twisted inside-out. The club had been watching Ronaldo and I think they concluded negotiations after the game. We always joked that Sheasy sealed the deal because he played like a f★★★ing clown against him."

Ronaldo enjoyed playing against Bolton over the years scoring six goals with four assists in nine further games. Yet, it took Ronaldo four years to register ten league goals in a single season - something he has comfortably achieved every year since, and a lot more. It turned out to be a disappointing season for United, who couldn't keep pace with Arsenal's Invincibles at the top of the table and surrendered their crown. Chelsea, who'd just been taken over by Roman Abramovich, finished second. In the end third-placed United finished 15 points behind the Gunners. They suffered a disappointing exit to Jose Mourinho's Porto in the last-16 of the Champions League. However much it pained Fergie to surrender the title, he did land the FA Cup, beating Millwall 3-0 in the final at

Cardiff, Ronaldo scored six goals in 40 games across all competitions – including a header in the FA Cup final.

As for that unforgettable debut, 'There's only one Ronaldo,' chanted the home fans at the final whistle; the same fans that had given his Brazilian namesake a standing ovation after a hat-trick there for Real Madrid a few months earlier.

MAN UNITED 4-0 BOLTON
FA Premiership; August 16, 2003

Manchester United: Tim Howard; Phil Neville, Quinton Fortune, Rio Ferdinand, Mikael Silvestre; Ole Gunnar Solskjaer (Eric Djemba-Djemba 67), Roy Keane, Nicky Butt (Cristiano Ronaldo 61), Ryan Giggs (Diego Forlan 80); Paul Scholes; Ruud van Nistelrooy
Substitutes not used: Roy Carroll (GK); John O'Shea
Manager: Sir Alex Ferguson
Scorers: Giggs 35, 73; Scholes 77; Van Nistelrooy 86

Bolton Wanderers: Jussi Jaaskelainen; Nicky Hunt, Florent Laville, Bruno N'Gotty, Ricardo Gardner, Stelios Giannakopoulos (Delroy Facey 76), Jay-Jay Okocha, Ivan Campo, Kevin Nolan (Per Frandsen 72), Henrik Pedersen (Youri Djorkaeff 59), Kevin Davies
Substitutes not used: Kevin Poole, Anthony Barness
Manager: Sam Allardyce
Booked: N'Gotty, Giannakopoulos, Nolan, Gardner
Attendance: 67,647
Referee: Paul Durkin (Dorset)

3: HOW THE DEAL WAS DONE

Cristiano Ronaldo had first asked his agent, Jorge Mendes, to sound out potential suitors as he prepared to return for pre-season training in mid-July under new head coach Massimiliano Allegri. Having signed a four-year contract worth an eye watering 31m a season after tax when he moved from Real Madrid to Juve in 2018, he was eager to pursue a new challenge after Portugal's exit in the last-16 of Euro 2020, as he was disillusioned with life in Turin.

Mendes approached Europe's big hitters, the ones who could afford his lavish salary. Even a move back to Madrid wouldn't be ruled out, but the most likely destinations were Paris Saint-Germain, both Manchester clubs and Chelsea.

Initially Mendes received little encouragement about a potential move, as quite often such approaches are usually seen as manoeuvring to improve terms and conditions at the club they are already at. In fact, Ronaldo released a statement criticising what he called "frivolous" speculation over his future on 18 August after reports in Spain linked him with a return to Madrid. "My story at Real Madrid has been written. It's been recorded. In words and numbers, in trophies and titles, in records and in headlines," he wrote on Instagram. While that seemed to rule out a return to the Bernabeu, it was also interpreted as a dampener for any pursuit by any other club.

Nevertheless within days Manchester City emerged as a potential suitor - they could afford him. When City's move for Spurs and England captain Harry Kane ended when Tottenham refused to budge on their £150m valuation it seemed obvious to all that a move for Ronaldo was the next logical step. However not all of City's hierarchy were convinced about the 36-year-old as it would be a departure from the club's policy of focussing on recruiting younger players. Nevertheless Mendes was confident of sealing a deal despite City's reluctance to pay a transfer fee. Once it became clear Juve would relinquish Ronaldo there were three days of intense negotiations between Mendes, City and Juventus.

Ronaldo requested a meeting with new head coach Massimiliano Allegri the day before Juve were due to face Udinese on Sunday in their first Serie A match of the season to inform him that he wanted to leave the club. They decided that he would start the match on the bench with Allegri introducing him in the 59th minute as a substitute for Álvaro Morata as Udinese walked off with a 2-2 draw.

Yet publically at least the Italian club maintained that Ronaldo was going nowhere with Juventus vice-president Pavel Nedved dismissing reports that he was set to leave, "we mustn't try to create sensational stories where there aren't any, I can absolutely confirm Ronaldo will remain at Juventus this season."

While Juve were determined to keep Ronaldo it became increasingly unlikely that they would unless they kept him against his will, meanwhile behind the scenes Mendes began negotiating with City but the reigning Premier League champions remained entrenched in their stubborn refusal to pay any sort of transfer fee. Mendes then had "a really tense" meeting with the Juventus sporting director Federico Cherubini during which Juve demanded a fee of

30m to balance their books to comply with financial fair play regulations. Cherubini had replaced Fabio Paratici in the role after his move to Tottenham earlier in the summer and did not enjoy such a strong relationship with Mendes as his predecessor.

Nevertheless City were confident Mendes could persuade Juve to negotiate a player exchange rather than a fee for Ronaldo City and made Raheem Sterling and Bernardo Silva available for transfer to balance their books but Juve rejected City's proposal and were prepared to hold onto Ronaldo unless a transfer fee was agreed. As a result Mendes spent Thursday morning trying to convince both parties to compromise but when no agreement could be struck Mendes, in pure frustration, contacted United.

At this point Ronaldo thought he was on his way to City as he assumed the hours of talks would bring some conclusion, but then he received a series of calls from Ronaldo's current and former team-mates including Bruno Fernandes and Rio Ferdinand. Ferdinand played with Ronaldo for six years and they had stayed in touch.

Crucially a personal intervention from his old boss Sir Alex clinched the deal. Ronaldo's father, Jose Dinis Aveiro, had died in 2005 and ever since Ferguson has been a father figure. On the day of Fergie's retirement, Ronaldo tweeted: "Thanks for everything, Boss." It was accompanied by a picture of Ferguson next to an 18-year-old Ronaldo at his United unveiling. Five months after he suffered a brain haemorrhage, Fergie went to the Crowne Plaza Hotel where Juve were staying ahead of their Champions League group stage tie with United in October 2018, to catch up with Ronaldo. "A great coach and above all a wonderful man," Ronaldo tweeted. "Taught me so many things inside and outside the pitch. Great to see you in good shape, Boss!"

The plot to wrest Ronaldo from the clutches of City continued as the player started to receive numerous calls urging him to 'come home' and, after talks with City had completely broken down, United moved in. In what will go down as one of the tensest weeks there has ever been in Manchester football United were suddenly in pole position but for supporters the rumours of Ronaldo being off to their hated rivals was too much to bear. Social media was awash with City fans gloating that they had 'bought' United's hero, arguably their best player since George Best. City fans were in hysterics at the prospect of taking one of United's most iconic players responsible for some of the greatest moments in the club's recent history. After a sleepless night, in which most reds tossed and turned hoping the rumours were false, Friday dawned with City still apparently in pole position while the few optimistic rumours emerging on twitter claiming that United had made a late bid to foil the deal were generally ignored.

All that changed during Ole Gunnar Solskjaer's a press conference ahead of the club's game with Wolves. Instead of a flat and well-rehearsed 'he isn't our player' response to direct questions Ole paused and prevaricated – a giveaway that something was afoot. Solskjaer tried some divisive tactics, he talked about his former team-mate who posed for a picture with his kids at Cardiff in 2014. Mike McGrath of The Daily Telegraph asked "With one of the greatest players ever on the market, why would Manchester United not try for a player like that?" The manager replied, "I didn't think Cristiano was gonna turn out leaving Juventus, and it's been speculation this morning and the last few days.

We've always had good communication. I know Bruno's been talking to him as well and he knows what we feel about him. And if he was ever gonna move away from Juventus he knows we're here." Immediately it seemed United were not only back in the game but favourites to re-sign their former legend.

Unbeknown to supporters negotiations continued between United and Juve were well advanced, an initial offer of 12m Euros was rejected but the Italian club eventually settled for 15m Euros up front and bonuses that could reach up to 8m with a guarantee of 20m. United and Mendes had already reached a verbal agreement over personal terms for a two-year contract as early as Thursday night at about the time United fans were panicking over seeing their former talisman in a Sky Blue shirt!

"[Ronaldo] gave his contribution, he made himself available, now he leaves and life goes on," boss Massimiliano Allegri said, "Things change, it's a law of life. Juventus remains, which is the most important thing. He is to be thanked for what he has done, also as an example among the youngsters. But as I said, we must go on." Ronaldo drove to the Juventus training ground, the Vinovo, to collect his belongings and inform Allegri and his teammates he was off to Manchester. That would not have come as much of a shock. What did come as a huge surprise that that it was United rather than City! United had set up a medical in Madrid to push the transfer through as quickly as possible and personal terms of £480,000-a week were quickly agreed. Juventus had paid a £99.2m transfer fee in July 2018 and on his departure in an Instagram post, he wrote, "Today I depart from an amazing club, the biggest in Italy and surely one of the biggest in all of Europe. I gave my heart and soul for Juventus and I'll always love the city of Turin until my final days."

So finally, after many years and several abortive attempts, it took the football world by surprise given that he had seemed destined to join United's bitter rivals. The attraction for United's owners, the Glazer family, was that Ronaldo would instantly get supporters back onside. Ronaldo became the club's third major signing of the summer following the arrivals of Jadon Sancho and Raphael Varane. Expectation levels had gone through the proverbial roof.

Later that Friday the official announcement was made, in a statement Manchester United said, "We are delighted to confirm that the club has reached agreement with Juventus for the transfer of Cristiano Ronaldo, subject to agreement of personal terms, visa and medical. Cristiano, a five-time Ballon d'Or winner, won five UEFA Champions League titles, four FIFA Club World Cups, seven league titles in England, Spain and Italy, and the European Championship for his native Portugal. In his first spell for Manchester United, he scored 118 goals in 292 games. Everyone at the club looks forward to welcoming Cristiano back to Manchester. He was also a European Championship winner with Portugal in 2016 and winner of 32 trophies for club and country with Sporting Lisbon, Manchester United, Real Madrid, Juventus and Portugal."

So Ronaldo agreed to return to United where he spent six years and won three Premier League titles, one Champions League, two League Cups and one FA Cup - as well as the Fifa Club World Cup and Community Shield - under Sir Alex Ferguson. At 4.51pm, the United Twitter account threatened to crash the clubs site. Eventually it did. The official United website crashed that evening as demand for tickets to the club's next two home games against Newcastle and West Ham went through the roof.

United referred to Ronaldo's 'offers/interest from multiple clubs', but did not specify City, but it tasted even sweeter that United had beaten City to such a stellar transfer. Rio Ferdinand said he had spoken to Ronaldo this week after reading reports linking him with a move to rivals Manchester City. He also said Ronaldo had spoken to former manager Sir Alex Ferguson before agreeing a return to Old Trafford. "Sir Alex played a massive part," Ferdinand said. "There was no way Cristiano was coming to Manchester United without speaking to Sir Alex. Simple as that. The attention on the club, the attention on the other players - you can't put into words what it's going to do for the dressing room and the fan base. He'll get you 25-30 goals this season. That's what he does - he outscored Romelu Lukaku last year in Serie A, but what he can do for Mason Greenwood, Marcus Rashford and Jadon Sancho alone is worth bringing. He will show them what an A-lister, genuine superstar and an absolute obsessive professional lives and breathes on a daily basis."

Speaking before Manchester City faced Arsenal that weekend in the Premier League manager Pep Guardiola said, "Cristiano is a Juventus player. I cannot add anything else. In these three or four days left until the transfer window shuts anything can happen but, in my view, there are few players - Cristiano Ronaldo included, Messi is another - they decide where they are going to play. Right now, my feeling is I am more than delighted with the squad we have and we will stay the same."

Speaking on BBC Radio 5 Live, Michael Owen was among a multitude of former players who added their weight to the argument that this transfer would transform United. The former England striker made it clear that United needed a centre-forward who can "bang in 25-plus goals a season; they haven't had that for a while. He's not a signing to appease the fans, he will be playing in all the big games. He definitely has a year or two more in him where he can score more than 20 goals. If he could score 30 goals this season I would be lost for words, but I wouldn't put anything past him, even now."

Owen Hargreaves, who won the Champions League alongside Ronaldo in 2008, said: "I remember my first day training with him. He was the first person on the training pitch, the first person in the ice bath and then the first person in the gym. I remember him doing sit-ups and at the end of his set he sat up and said: 'I'm going to be the best player in the world at the end of this year.' And he was. His dedication to his craft is equal to his talent, which is remarkable. Everyone thinks it's all about him, but he wants to win. He's coming back to United to win and that's why I think as a mentor for these young guys at United he is the perfect fit and I think it's going to be fabulous to watch it all."

Yet the transfer saga alone was one of the most incredible any one could remember and in terms of Manchester's two big clubs it seemed to be a power-shift back to the red side with City prevaricating over signing him when they clearly needed a striker. For United fans it was as much a relief to see him not going to the blue side as it was exciting to see him back in a red shirt. All eyes were now on his potential home debut against Newcastle United and the hysteria would only grow in the coming weeks during the international break.

4: RONALDO'S RETURN

"It was like Caesar entering Rome after victory. 'I came, I saw, I conquered'. It was fantastic!"

SIR ALEX FERGUSON

As the Sky Sports News transfer deadline day countdown clock ticked down to zero, former Arsenal and England midfielder Paul Merson started to question Cristiano Ronaldo's return to Manchester United. He was far from alone questioning whether Ronaldo's return was a wise move. Merson couldn't argue with Ronaldo retaining a stunning physique but he felt that his legs couldn't carry him past defenders as they used to at the age of 36. Merson argued that Ronaldo wouldn't have the stamina to work backwards to help defend, so the team would effectively be playing with ten men!

"His physique is great," Merson admitted, "Everyone can keep themselves in shape – it's the legs. He is not going to be able to run past too many people and that is the problem. They are going to say: 'You stay up front, we'll put the ball in the box and you've got to score. When they haven't got the ball, they've got ten players."

Merson's point was that the pace of the Premier League was much faster than the league he left behind and that in his twelve years in Spain and Italy he had become used to a more sedate version of the game. Merson didn't think he could adapt, given his age, to English football that had become so much faster, more demanding and a lot more intense. Merson also felt that Ronaldo is "not the same player" as he was in his first, explosive spell at United.

However his former Arsenal team-mate Ian Wright believed that one United star could become a frightening prospect if he learns from Ronaldo - Mason Greenwood. Sir Alex Ferguson had already pointed out that the Bradford-born attacker is one of the best youngsters to come through the club's academy and has already been capped by England at senior level. Wright believed that Ronaldo's return would be a massive boost to the forward, "the only thing I can equate Ronaldo's return to is just knowing that Dennis Bergkamp was coming for us at Arsenal and how that changed us. I cannot even get into the realms of thinking what that is going to do for their academy players, especially someone like Greenwood. He can just watch now. Cristiano Ronaldo will probably want to impart and tell him what he needs to do."

Greenwood scored in each of his side's three games at the start of the new season, but could see his place taken by Ronaldo against Newcastle. "I was speaking to Sir Alex the other day. We were playing golf and he mentioned about Mason Greenwood being one of the best they've ever had out of their academy," added Wright, "now you put one of the best players that's ever played for the football club. He's come back as a world icon to play with him and alongside him it's frightening what this guy could turn into. The mentality of him rubbing off on people could be the difference for Manchester United."

Within the United camp there was a vastly different. Paul Pogba was excited by the arrivals of Ronaldo and Raphael Varane in particular and felt that the new signing was "going to raise the level" at United ahead of a challenging Premier League season, "It's always a pleasure to play with the best. It's also a plus for the players to be able to train with a great player. He's going to raise the level of the team. Everybody knows [what Ronaldo brings]. He's already a legend in this club and he's coming back, so obviously it's huge for us, for the club. He's going to bring his experience, his quality and obviously when he comes the level [of the team] goes up."

John O'Shea was one of many former United contingent to be buzzing along with Gary Neville about Ronaldo's impending arrival. "Although you could see he was at the beginning of his journey when he came to United, he was a super intelligent boy and realised what he was able to do. He wasn't the finished article when he left for Madrid, but the numbers he's reached since then are scary. The day it was confirmed that he was coming back to United was an incredible feeling. My phone was bouncing everywhere with messages. It just made everyone so happy. United fans and everyone associated with the club, and even fans of other clubs thought it was amazing to see Ronaldo back in the Premier League. The young kids at United will be absolutely buzzing. Now it's the real business and he still has the goods - as Ireland unfortunately found out in the international break. That's why United have signed him, and I'm sure he's going to show that this season."

Sir Alex Ferguson was never going to allow Manchester City to capture Ronaldo when it became clear he was leaving Juve. At one stage Ronaldo looked to be on his way to Pep Guardiola's side, but Fergie, Rio Ferdinand, Bruno Fernandes and others made calls insisting that Cristiano return to Old Trafford instead. They refused to countenance Ronaldo joining their Manchester rivals. "I couldn't imagine him playing for Manchester City – I don't think anybody could," Ferguson said, "that's why we made steps to ensure that he came here. The club then followed him well, I spoke to the Glazers, and then it was done." Ferguson stressed that many parties at Old Trafford were involved in bringing the five-time Ballon d'Or winner back to the club. Sir Alex said: "A lot of people played their part. I contributed a bit, but really Cristiano really wanted to come here, that was important – it worked very well."

There was no one prouder to witness his second coming than the former manager who brought him to the club in the first place, "It's fantastic. You saw that on Saturday, it was like Caesar entering Rome after victory. 'I came, I saw, I conquered'. It was fantastic. I mean, for anyone who is a United fan, we could have had a million people in there, without doubt, as there were so many outside, hundreds outside. It's one of these things. When he was here as a kid, his learning process was very, very quick. A lot of people said he was a diver and there was a little spell of that but, after that, he was attacking defenders and all he needed was a nudge and he would waltz by them. He would attack with unbelievable speed. I think the increasing knowledge of his game - I think he was born with a desire. He sacrificed himself to be the best."

Rio Ferdinand opened up on how he joined Sir Alex in the charm offensive to persuade Ronaldo to ditch a lucrative move to City to return to United. The former United defender put in a call to his former team-mate. "We spoke and I'm just pleased he's where he's at. The idea that he was going to put on a Manchester City shirt was the stuff of bad dreams." Rio agreed with his former boss that Ronaldo would have a huge influence on emerging young talent within the team especially. "I had Neil Ruddock," he told Sportsmail while discussing his own early influences in his career, "They get Cristiano Ronaldo and I get Neil Ruddock! Unbelievable. Neil's a great guy but they're different professionals, if you know what I mean!"

Greenwood was one of the young strikers who would benefit from a footballing education alongside Ronaldo and would help Rashford rekindle his sparkle. Ole Gunnar Solskjaer splashed out £73million on Jadon Sancho, and he too would be lifted by playing alongside Ronaldo.

As usual there were some pundits looking at the negatives with some suggesting that such young talent would find their pathway to the first team blocked by Ronaldo's arrival. It was not a theory that Rio subscribed to − "If I'm Rashford and Greenwood, I'm the happiest kid on the planet right now. They have the opportunity to work with someone like Cristiano that you never thought would have been possible, someone ambitious and ridiculous. I think they have to be like sponges, they have to be students. They have to watch him. I'd become obsessed with him if I was a kid there. It doesn't matter what position you're playing in but if you're a striker, then you're obsessed. I'd be watching him thinking 'I'm a weirdo' because you want to just know and see what he does to be the best and stay at the top there for so many years.'

Ronaldo was the golden boy in one of United's greatest eras, with Ferdinand alongside Nemanja Vidic in a rock solid defence, and that is the area that United needed to get right to ensure their abundance of attacking talent had the right back up. The arrival of Raphael Varane from Real Madrid for £42m addresses that issue to a large extent. "There's good players all over the pitch, players can come in during certain games and do jobs," argued Rio. "That's what you want, especially in the back four. Lindelof can come in for a game here or there, I'd be more than okay with that. Dalot's staying at right-back, he had a good season with AC Milan. Telles can come in for Shaw, you've got back-ups everywhere. We've definitely got the personnel to challenge on all fronts and they've got the squad depth now. They've added one world class player (in Ronaldo) and another potentially world class player (in Sancho). They certainly have a better opportunity to challenge for the Champions League than they have done in recent years.'

5: RONALDO'S PLEDGE

"This is absolutely 100% the stuff that dreams are made of!"

CRISTIANO RONALDO

I n the first comments, press releases and interviews, Ronaldo made it clear that this move was not about him in particular, but it was all about his desire for more glory, more trophies, and his desire to make it happen. It was a megastar talking up the team ethic, despite the fact that an expectant Theatre of Dreams were dreaming of his goals, and his star quality. Cristiano vowed that "history will be written once again" it genuinely appeared that he wasn't back in Manchester to tickle his own ego but to deliver the goods in terms of silverware, especially at the highest level – namely the title and the Champions league which was not just elusive in recent years, but, realistically, way out of sight.

Having completed his return it was fair to say it was an emotional experience. So many players are little more than mercenaries drifting from club to club, country to country, but it was clear that Old Trafford pulled on his heart strings as well as his bank balance. Then again he had become one of football's first billionaires. His 'homecoming' after 12 years away after departing for Real Madrid back in 2009 was officially confirmed with Ronaldo sending a lengthy and passionate message to fans on Instagram. In doing so, Ronaldo mentioned his memorable first stint at the club as he described his return as "like a dream come true". He signed off the post by dedicating his return Sir Alex, who played an integral part in making the deal happen after personally interceding when interest from rivals Manchester City first emerged.

Ronaldo wrote: " Everyone who knows me, knows about my never ending love for Manchester United. The years I spent in this club where absolutely amazing and the path we've made together is written in gold letters in the history of this great and amazing institution. I can't even start to explain my feelings right now, as I see my return to Old Trafford announced worldwide. It's like a dream come true, after all the times that I went back to play against Man. United, and even as an opponent, to have always felt such love and respect from the supporters in the stands. This is absolutely 100% the stuff that dreams are made of! My first domestic League, my first Cup, my first call to the Portuguese National team, my first Champions League, my first Golden Boot and my first Ballon d'Or, they were all born from this special connection between me and the Red Devils. History has been written in the past and history will be written once again! You have my word! I'm right here! I'm back where I belong! Let's make it happen once again! PS - Sir Alex, this one is for you…"

That sign off virtually confirmed that one of the reasons for his return, possibly the main one, was that Sir Alex was still at Old Trafford, and remained influential within the club. Ronaldo made it clear ahead of meeting up with his new team-mates for the first time at the Carrington training camp once he completes a five-day quarantine period. He told them 'I'm here to win' passing on the message via his Portuguese team-mate Bruno Fernandes. It was viewed as a confidence booster for the entire squad, with hopes raised that they could challenge for the title and even the Champions League. The place was buzzing.

Yet despite the addition of world-class talent, Rio Ferdinand remained sceptical of the club's chances of reigning supreme in Europe as they had when he played alongside Ronaldo. Rio argued that Manchester City and Chelsea possessed squads that had already gained the valuable experience of having won major trophies and with that comes greater belief. Liverpool also fell into that category of tasting title and Champions League victories in recent times and would again be one of the teams to beat with squads in terms of experience as a group were still "way ahead of us". "In terms of experience and know-how, right now United are starting at the bottom of the pack in terms of the favourites. I'd put them behind Liverpool, Chelsea and Man City. You then look at Paris Saint-Germain, they've had an unbelievable window, one of the best I've ever seen and Bayern Munich will also be there or thereabouts so because of the weakness of the Spanish teams now I think it'll be Bayern, PSG and two English teams in the semis.'

United, though, now had Ronaldo, and Rio was sure he could replicate the form of his first Old Trafford stint. 'People keep saying, he's not this, he's not that - but he was top goalscorer in Serie A last season. Everyone saying he's dropped in quality but he's still better than everyone else. I expect him to be nearer 25 to 30 goals this season, at least in all competitions. If he doesn't get to 30 I'll be surprised.'

Ronaldo had failed to reach 30 goals in all competitions just once since he left United in 2009 and Paul Pogba explained the way Ronaldo influenced the dressing room atmosphere from the very start. Ronaldo returned to Old Trafford from Juve just like Pogba did five years earlier.

Now they would play on the same side for the first time in their careers. Pogba wanted to compete with the biggest honours in world football and was keeping his options open during the final year of his United contract, linked with moves to Paris Saint-Germain and Real Madrid. Ronaldo might influence his future contract talks. After failing to win a title or Champions League during his time back in Manchester, Pogba was convinced to move on, but now it might change with Ronaldo's arrival depending how it all panned out success as well as a new contract offer. "It's always a pleasure to play with the best, it's a plus for the players to be able to train with a great player. He's going to raise the level of the team." The 28-year-old added on Sky Sports before the deal was finalised: "Everybody knows [what he brings]. He's already a legend in this club and he's coming back, so obviously it's huge for us, for the club. He's going to bring his experience, his quality and obviously when he comes the level [of the team] goes up."

According to Pogba, the signing of France team-mate Raphael Varane, who spent seven years at Real Madrid with Ronaldo, would have a similar effect at the other end of the pitch, "Raph's arrival is a positive for the club, we have a great relationship, we've known each other for a while. I'm happy that he's with us at Manchester to bring his experience and quality to the table."

Yet Paul Merson stuck to his guns ahead of Ronaldo's opening match. "He's just not going to be the player that beats players," the pundit said. "You watch them when he was at Man United before he was extraordinary. The stuff he was doing, step-overs... my telly fell off the stand once, the camera man went, the lot. He was just that good. He will score you goals if you put the ball in the box, Ronaldo needs crosses in my opinion. You've seen it against the Republic of Ireland, put it in the box the man, he's a finisher, they play with two wingers who don't cross the ball. They play with Sancho who cuts inside and has a shot, Greenwood on the other side who wants to come inside or even go outside like he did against Wolves and have shots." Merson pointed out that Juventus did not look like winning the Champions League, despite that being the main reason for Ronaldo's 2018 arrival. He insisted that winning the Premier League would be the "biggest thing" in the forward's career. But he added: "If Man City had come in for him, he wouldn't be at Man Utd."

Ronaldo flew in by private jet for his Manchester United return and immediately felt at home in a multi-million pound mansion. His plane touched down at the city's airport at 5.40pm on Thursday after travelling from Faro. He was met on the runway by United officials and a security team and the awaiting media watched as he was whisked away to a luxury seven-bedroom countryside hideaway with a high-tech fitness complex including pool and jacuzzi — allowing him to top up his fitness. A six-strong security team accompanied him and patrolled the property, which the club rented.

Ronaldo arrived in Manchester 24 hours before his 27-year-old partner Georgina Rodriguez posted a series of photos on Instagram of her and their four children travelling by private jet. The pictures carried a heart emoji above the Manchester location tag. She also posted a picture of a "welcome" Cadbury's chocolate bar bearing the Manchester United logo. Georgina previously worked in the UK as a nanny before moving to Spain and meeting him.

Ronaldo's minders were pictured collecting a meal for him at a restaurant in Alderley Edge, Cheshire. Ronaldo spent five days in quarantine before going to United's Carrington training ground to meet his new team-mates with the media speculating that he brought with him the message that he wanted them to win the league in his first season back.

Despite the shortage of preparation time he felt fit and sharp and ready to start instantly in the team after games with Portugal. Ronaldo scored twice including a 96th-minute winner in a World Cup qualifier against the Republic of Ireland.

Cristiano's mum Dolores Aveiro flew to Manchester to link up with her son and posted a photo of herself flying in a private jet towards the UK to join him and his family. Dolores shared the pic on Instagram with the caption: "On the way to Manchester, kisses everyone!"

Ronaldo announced his delight at reclaiming the No 7 shirt when he said: "I'm really glad and looking forward to starting my first game." There had been speculation for days over which number he would wear. Ronaldo famously wore the number 7 shirt throughout his career, but Edinson Cavani possessed the coveted shirt over the past year when he became one of the most popular members of the team with supporters due to his work ethic and goals. The Uruguayan accumulated 17 goals in all competitions and now opted for the No 21 shirt, which was left vacant by Daniel James who signed for Leeds for £25million. Cavani wears that number for his country. Ronaldo praised his new team-mate with a thank you message. "I wasn't sure if it would be possible to have the number seven shirt again," said Ronaldo in a statement. "So I would like to say a huge thank you to Edi for this incredible gesture."

Ronaldo Jnr is better than his dad, according to his grandma. Dolores Aveiro believes her grandson is 'better than his father was at his age' because he has his dad as a teacher. Cristiano 'Cristianinho' Ronaldo Jr is already taking the first tentative steps in following his fathers' footsteps and the 11-year-old is already looking to play for Sporting Lisbon in the future. 'Ronaldo has to come back here [to Sporting], for me he'd be here,' Aveiro said on the ADN de Leao podcast. 'He likes to watch Sporting's games. I've already told him: "Son, before I die I want to see you return to Sporting". "Let's see...", he said, but if it isn't [him], it's Cristianinho! At his age, he plays better than Ronaldo. At the time, Ronaldo didn't have a coach, but today Ronaldo is his son's teacher.'

Cristianinho is Ronaldo's eldest son and he has already been training with his father at Manchester United after spending two years at Juventus' academy. At the Turin club, Cristiano Ronaldo Jr was quite impressive for the Under 9s, scoring 56 goals in 35 games, with 26 assists last year. Ronaldo will support anything his boy wants to do, and would love to see him become a footballer. 'I would love for him to be a footballer, because he feels passion for this sport,' Ronaldo told DAZN. 'He is a competitor and he hates losing.' Sounds familiar!

Ronaldo's impact on the United squad was instant with goalkeeper Lee Grant joking that his team-mates opted out of their usual tasty desserts after seeing the new signing's healthy dinner. 38-year-old Grant told talkSPORT that his team-mates would normally tuck into a sweet treat after dinner when they eat at the hotel the night before a match but having observed eating regime and seeing him tuck into quinoa, avocado and boiled eggs, not one of them wanted dessert after the meal. Lee explained: "You finish your dinner and usually on a Friday night you've got a few cheat stuff out. You've got a bit of apple crumble and custard or you've got a bit of brownie and cream. I tell you now, not one player touched the apple crumble and custard, not one player went up for that brownie. We were sat down on our table for table pre-match and straight away one of the lads said to me 'what has Cristiano got on his plate? We were having a little gander over at what he's got and obviously it's the cleanest, most healthy plate you could imagine. It just cracked me up how not one player got up to take that junk food on which was laid out."

Ole Gunnar Solskjaer later suggested Grant might have been over egging it a little saying. "That's obviously a joke by Granty in a setting with some mates, it's not as though we were eating junk food before he came in and he's changed it all but obviously he's proved how to look after yourself. He's an example for other players how to prolong your career. It's the best time of your life, so stay in the game as long as you can. Be professional. When you're done, you can let yourself go as I have done now!'

Ronaldo's ability to stay in peak condition at the age of 36 was something that the football world had been discussing for some time, and it had been widely reported that he eats up to six meals a day, avoids harmful processed food and red meat and instead had a stable diet of fish, notably swordfish, tuna and braised cod as particular favourites. He regards chicken as 'magical' because of its high protein content and low fat, and will often eat ham and cheese and low-fat yoghurt for breakfast. No doubt the Lisbon speciality of Bacalao a la Brasa would be one of his favourite meals - a mixture of braised cod, onions, thinly sliced potatoes and scrambled eggs.

Ronaldo has eight hours sleep a night and can sometimes take up to as many as five naps during the day. He has spoken about the importance of sleep when he said: "Proper sleep is really important for getting the most out of training. I go to bed early and get up early, especially before matches. Sleep helps muscles recover which is really important."

Maintaining mental health is another of Ronaldo's priorities for his ability to stay at the top for longer, and that it is just as important as his physical wellbeing. "Training and physical sessions are most important, but living a relaxed lifestyle helps you to be the best you can be, physically and mentally. I spend my free time with family and friends, which keeps me relaxed and in a positive mindset." Maintaining that vital balance means he spends quality time with his family - partner Georgina Rodriguez and his four children Cristiano Jr, twins Mateo and Eva Maria and Alana Martina.

Troy Deeney was not surprised that Cristiano's team-mates followed his example and avoided sweet treats and desserts due to the admiration they have for his career with the former Watford striker claiming that if, "he ate horses★★t for a pre-match meal, I'd eat horses★★t too!"

Within days of moving into his Cheshire mansion he was forced to move because sheep in the fields behind his house kept him awake. There was also a security issue, which is more likely to have been the real reason for the quick re housing. He switched his seven-bedroom, £6m house in Cheshire with 23 acres of land for a £3m one owned by former United star Andrew Cole. The first property was set in rolling fields but near a field full of sheep it also had a public footpath across the land and the road at the front gave a view inside the property. Ronaldo, who places a lot of emphasis on rest and recovery after games, decided it was best if he moved. His new mansion comes with a pool, cinema and a garage big enough for four cars, plus CCTV cameras, electric gates and security guards on patrol. Ronaldo lived close by during his previous stint at United so it felt like home. His kids were in a private school and once the hysteria of his return dies down, he could take Georgina out and show her his favourite local spots.

Ronaldo doesn't cook and is not very good at DIY, according to partner Georgina Rodriquez. The model, who has been in a relationship with him since 2017 and joined him in England after he returned to Old Trafford along with their four children. The 27-year-old gave an insight into her relationship in an interview with an Italian magazine, "Cristiano is a super dad and the best husband I could dream of but he doesn't cook. After training all morning, he deserves to find a good plate of hot food prepared with love at the table. We have a chef and sometimes I cook."

Rodriguez banned him from changing any light bulbs or any other in-house hazardous chores in their house to avoid unnecessary injuries. Rodriguez does it instead or brings in someone to do it for them! "Changing a light bulb in our house is impossible, we have such high ceilings.

If you were Cristiano Ronaldo, would you change a light bulb nearly 20 foot above the ground? Better not. Take care of yourself and dedicate yourself to being the best at what you do. I'll take care of the rest. I make it all work out. I like to take care of my home and my family."

6: TWO-GOAL SECOND DEBUT

"I have not come back to be a cheerleader. If you guys want to succeed, then I need you to love this club from the bottom of your hearts."

CRISTIANO RONALDO

Ole Gunnar Solskjaer was delighted that his new signing gave a powerful and inspiring speech to his squad the night before the big game 'homecoming' as the entire group of players and coaching staff listened in silence. In it the new signing told the squad that he had returned to United for two reasons, firstly because he loved the club and secondly he loves the winning mentality that breeds through the ranks of this club. He went on to tell his team-mates that he had not come back to be a cheerleader and told them that if they wanted to succeed, then he needed them to love this club from the bottom of their hearts. They needed to eat, sleep and fight for United whether they played or not and support your team-mates and always give 100 per cent. "I am here to win and nothing else. Winning brings us happiness. I want to be happy, do you?" he asked his team-mates, "I watched as United had struggled over the past few years following the departure of Sir Alex Ferguson. The club has taken a fall. But I believe in you and that you have enough talent to bring back winning ways. You are all amazing players and I believe in you, or else I would have not returned. The fans will support you, if you give your best. I just want to create a winning mentality, so when I do retire one day, the winning mentality will remain, and this group of players will dominate football, like we did in the past. I will do my best for the team but I need your support too. Are you ready to fight? Are you ready to leave everything on the pitch?" It was a powerful, inspiring speech and his team-mates gave him a round of applause at the end.

Former United captain Bryan Robson was aware that Ronaldo addressed the players on Friday night and that he would emphasise that he was back at the club to win, "he's not here for a fairytale that ends in failure". Robson has experienced plenty of players with a lot to say for themselves about their achievements, but with Ronaldo, his record speaks for itself, it is second to none, and that speaks volumes. "You know it really hurts him to lose and he'll have no qualms telling you. That is something others will thrive off."

Robson felt such positivity will reflect on improved performances for Jadon Sancho who he felt could be braver and was so far playing within himself, which was not to be unexpected coming to a new club and coming from a different pace of football in Germany. Robson felt the manager now had a really strong group with quality in every position and with that comes the demand for success. "Pressure is always there as manager of Manchester United, Ole knows he will have to win trophies and at the very least get closer to the Premier League title than last year." Robson felt the key was how the relatively inexperienced manager would deal with so many strong personalities within that United dressing room

Robson had been talking with his old boss Sir Alex Ferguson who excelled at dealing with strong characters within the United dressing room from Eric Cantona to

Roy Keane, "Sir Alex wasn't bothered about upsetting players at times because it was always schemed to bring the best out of them. I'm really keen to see how Ole steps up with this squad now. How he freshens them up in the cups, how he develops the formations and strategies to beat teams, when to make his substitutions and who to bring on to make the best attacking impact because with the armoury United now possess, they will face a lot of sides who will be defensive in their approach. They will need to grind out results like they did at Wolves. Sides who can do that, collect a series of 1-0 wins, will win league titles. Chelsea are stronger, City are and so are Liverpool but there is no reason for United not to believe they can win it too. That's what Cristiano is here for."

Cristiano Ronaldo was capable of playing until he is 40-years-old and emulating the longevity of Ryan Giggs, according to former striker partner Wayne Rooney. On the eve of Ronaldo's second coming against Newcastle Rooney, now manager of Derby County, believed that his former team-mate had changed his game considerably which enabled him to stay at the very top. Rooney felt that when they played together in the United attack Ronaldo was more of a runner, a great dribbler, with pace and power but now he was as an out and out goalscorer.

Rooney, who is Manchester United's all-time top scorer, said "His ability is obviously one thing, but then he's also looked after himself massively... he's still in great condition. It wouldn't surprise me if he's playing until he's 40, like Ryan Giggs did, and still scoring goals." Wayne also felt his new team-mates will have to work a little harder. Rooney added: "But if it's anything like last time - towards the last two years of playing with him - the team allowed him to do that because he scores you goals, and goals win you games. With Cristiano it's different. The likes of Cristiano and Lionel Messi – probably only those two really – they only play in one half of the pitch. It's not box-to-box or high energy defending that uses your energy when you have the ball in one half of the pitch. It's all about scoring goals."

They might have been team-mates forging an exciting and formidable attack, but there is, of course, their infamous fall out, at least a row build up in the media, concedes while both at the World Cup representing their countries, and that famous Ronaldo wink. Now, though, Rooney concedes that getting sent off in the 2006 World Cup quarter-final was the 'worst feeling' he experienced in football, but he doesn't any blame toward Ronaldo. In fact, his moment of shame actually brought them closer together after clear-the-air talks in the tunnel after the game. England faced Portugal in Gelsenkirchen full of confidence against Portugal but ended up knocked out with Rooney red carded. It all kicked off on the hour as Rooney tangled with Ricardo Carvalho and stamped on the then-Chelsea defender and was dismissed by referee Horacio Elizondo after Ronaldo protested to the referee indicating that Rooney had to go. When the red card was brandished Ronaldo was captured by the TV cameras giving a cheeky wink to the Portuguese bench. Rooney recalled how the game was going alright for England until his red card. Rooney blamed his violent reaction to the referee not giving him a free kick when he was the victim of a clear foul by Ricardo Carvalho who was pulling and pushing him while Petit came in from the other side.

However Rooney didn't hold any grudges against

Ronaldo as he reassured his United team-mate at the time, "I've no issues with you. Enjoy your tournament and good luck. I'll see you in a few weeks — and let's go try and win the league."

Despite a tabloid frenzy ahead of United's first game of the season the pair dove-tailed superbly as United beat Fulham 5-1 with Rooney scoring two and setting the other up for Ronaldo which paved the way for United to win the league. "In the dressing room we were always really close. It was always the two of us doing pranks on the manager or other players. And what had happened brought us closer together on the pitch. The next three years were our best as a partnership and brought three titles and the Champions League. My red card in Gelsenkirchen was the starting point."

Ronaldo was jeered throughout the following campaign but refused to let it affect him as he still finished as the club's top scorer en route to winning the title. Yet if anything the incident served to create an 'us and them' mentality between United and the rest of English football which players and supporters turned into a huge motivating factor. As Ronaldo recalls, "The media created a big drama which never existed. So when I arrived back in England I was kind of afraid, not because of Rooney but because of England supporters. They made a huge story when I did the wink, but it was not because of the circumstances with Rooney, it was another situation. It was difficult timing for me because I thought when I arrived in Manchester, people were going to boo me in all the stadiums. But it's the past, I had a chat with Rooney when I arrived back in Manchester. We are still friends, we speak about that and he understands my point of view. Of course, he helped me in all circumstances. He said, 'Cristiano, this is the past, let's speak about the present, let's win trophies together'."

There was no doubt in Ronaldo's mind that he would be starting against Newcastle in his first game back insisting he was fully fit and ready to go. In fact he was going to be in the manager's ear to make sure Ole Gunnar Solskjaer made him part of the starting line up. "Of course I will be nervous on Saturday, but I am more mature, I am more experienced. I will be prepared and I am going to make pressure to Ole now to start me in the XI. I am ready to go!"

A shadow still hung over United's new signing as the 'Level Up' feminist group protested outside Old Trafford saying they wanted to "remind crowds" of rape allegations against him. Kathryn Mayorga claims she was assaulted by him at a Las Vegas hotel in 2009 when US prosecutors said Ronaldo, who denied the claims, would not face charges. A plane with the banner "Believe Kathryn Mayorga" was flown after the start of the game. Ms Mayorga had reportedly reached an out-of-court settlement with Ronaldo in 2010, involving a £288,000 ($375,000) payment for agreeing never to publicise the allegations. Ronaldo's lawyers have previously stated the non-disclosure agreement was "by no means a confession of guilt". They insisted he was following advice "to put an end to the outrageous accusations made against him, in order precisely to avoid attempts […] to destroy a reputation built thanks to hard work, athletic ability and behavioural correction". In 2018 Ms Mayorga sought to reopen the case, with her lawyer saying she had been inspired by the #MeToo movement against sexual violence. Las Vegas police, who then investigated the allegations, said they "cannot be proven beyond a reasonable doubt" and therefore they would not press charges against Ronaldo. A local district attorney's office said Ms Mayorga reported an assault in 2009 but refused to state where it had happened or name the attacker, so police were unable "to conduct any meaningful investigation".

Ronaldo has never denied that the two met but said the encounter, when he was about to leave his first United stint for Real Madrid, was consensual. He tweeted in 2018: "I firmly deny the accusations being issued against me. Rape is an abominable crime that goes against everything that I am and believe in." Level Up said they wanted to "disrupt the fanfare" around the player's heavily-publicised return to United. The group's co-director Janey Starling said they wanted to send "a message to football that rape allegations can't be kicked off the pitch".

It had been a tough few months for the Glazer family. The previous season had ended in farce with the Liverpool fixture having to be abandoned following the invasion of the stadium by supporters protesting against the European Super League and the club's American owners, who have taken over £1 billion out of the club since their 2005 takeover, being door-stepped by reporters in Florida. Yet the signing of Ronaldo seemed to have changed the atmosphere around the club at a stroke. Club owner Avram Glazer was at Old Trafford for the first time in two years to witness his new investment in action. Gary Oldman was another to cross the Atlantic and lend some Hollywood glamour to the directors' box. Ryan Giggs and Sir Alex Ferguson, involved in Ronaldo's first debut in August 2003, were in attendance, with Giggs joined by his son, Zach, a winger in the United academy.

The night before the game there was a dinner reunion for Steve Bruce and Bryan Robson, former team-mates at Old Trafford and Bryan knew the conversation would centre on Ronaldo's Return, and Bryan knew Steve would be shaking his head and wondering why he had the misfortune to be the opponent's for the hero's return. United legend Bryan Robson told Mail on Sunday that he had "not sensed a buzz around Old Trafford like this since Eric Cantona arrived". Robson felt like a fan when he turned up at the stadium at 11.45am and it was already packed outside.

Ronaldo rarely lets down his fans, and there are hundreds of millions worldwide, and this was no exception. Cheered from the moment he left the team coach on its arrival at the ground, throughout the warm-up and then once the game had started, Ronaldo repaid them in the best possible manner with two goals and broke the record for the longest gap between Premier League appearances - with 12 years and 118 days since his previous game for the Reds in May 2009. His first goal in 12 years for United was a gift, as Newcastle goalkeeper Freddie Woodman parried Mason Greenwood's deflected effort into his path, but as the TV replay showed in slow motion, the striker was the first out of the blocks, anticipating there might be a rebound, while others were flat footed, he was first to the ball to prod home from close range. A couple of minutes earlier, he had spurned a chance, albeit from a very tight angle as he misjudged his effort and ended up spooning the ball into the advertising hoardings. At 36 years, 218 days old, Ronaldo broke yet another record – he was the oldest player to score for United in the Premier League since Ryan Giggs in February 2013.

However the match was far from one way traffic as Newcastle had shown a willingness to break and could easily have taken an early lead through Joe Willock and they started the second half in positive fashion and hit back in the 56th minute with a strike from Javier Manquillo following a swift break. Yet just as United fans feared that their homecoming party might end in a huge anticlimax, Luke Shaw broke forward and played a wonderful through-ball put Ronaldo clear and his fellow Portuguese took a superb touch before hitting the ball through Woodman's legs. He recorded a speed of 20.2mph during the build up to his second goal, ranking him amongst the fastest players in the Premier League so far this season, food for thought for the likes of Paul Merson who had doubted him. Fernandes sealed the result for Solskjaer's side with a thunderous 25 yarder before Jesse Lingard finished off an intricate move in the 92nd minute to seal the points. There was to be no repeat of the hat-trick he scored on his last appearance against Newcastle at Old Trafford in January 2008.

Ole had coached Ronaldo, Rooney and Tevez and the United boss was proud whenever Cristiano or Rooney scored through a defender's legs, "I nudged [son] Noah and say: 'Your dad taught them that'".

It was the perfect day for United as they stormed to the top of the Premier League on a day to remember at Old Trafford. Ronaldo was the star of the show and the victory raised hopes that it would inspire Ole Gunnar Solskjaer to his first trophy at the club.

The atmosphere around Manchester that day had been nothing short of extraordinary, as Gary Neville "I walked out into Manchester's city centre on Saturday morning and I've not seen it as alive for five or 10 years. What he's done to the Premier League for interest is exciting but for the city, he's absolutely got it buzzing with excitement – and this was even before he scored the two goals. I was at Salford and saw the news that he scored. I could only imagine what the atmosphere was like and I spoke to a couple of people who were there and they said it was out of this world, bouncing like they've never seen it before and Salford scored in the last minute which meant it was the perfect football day. Everyone is talking about Cristiano Ronaldo and Manchester United, Manchester City being champions and Chelsea signing Romelu Lukaku, so everything has been away from Liverpool with people questioning if this team is over the hill or past their best. But this was a really good performance, they did everything they were asked to do.'

7: 'I WAS SUPER NERVOUS'

"I didn't expect to score two goals. I expect one but not two."

CRISTIANO RONALDO

It was almost an hour after the full-time whistle at Old Trafford when Cristiano Ronaldo finally emerged to do his post-match interviews pitch-side, but he was still greeted by cheers and songs from United supporters. A section of the crowd in the Stretford End and the Sir Bobby Charlton stand serenaded their old-new hero with chants of "Viva Ronaldo". Ronaldo described the reception as "incredible" and even admitted he was "super nervous". He didn't expect to score two goals, but he expected one if not two. "It was an unbelievable moment," for him.

Ronaldo does not come across as a player who feels nervous, he appears to be super confident with a massive ego but the reality is far different. He admitted that the mammoth anticipation for his Old Trafford return got to him. "It is unbelievable. When I started the game I was so nervous, I swear. It is normally because I did not expect that they would sing my name all game. I was very nervous but maybe I didn't show but I was. The reception is incredible but I am here to win games and help the team. It was unbelievable moment. I was super nervous and was thinking last night that I wanted to play good and show I was still capable of helping the team. This club is unbelievable and I am so proud. I am going to give everything to make them proud of me. Everyone knows the football in England is different than in any part of the world and to be honest it is the most special one. I arrived here at 18 and they treated my unbelievable and that is why I am back.

"I didn't expect to score two goals. I expect one but not two. I have to appreciate the fans and what they did to me today, I feel so proud for that. The most important thing was to win and to win games. Manchester needs to be where they deserve. It is to win, to build the team and build the club and the mentality. This is what we are looking for. Of course I am happy to score goals I am not going to deny that but the most important thing is the team and the team played good.

"When I started the game I was so nervous, I swear. But I think it was normal. I didn't expect they would sing all game my name so I was very nervous. Maybe it didn't show, but I was. The reception is incredible, but I'm here to win games, to help the team and get the club back where they deserve." The trademark self-confidence was in evidence, though, as he admitted he fully expected to see his name on the scoresheet. "Of course, I'm happy to score the goals, I won't deny that, but the most important thing is the team, that they play consistently, they play at a high level and most of the time, we showed a mature intelligence so I'm proud of that."

Manager Ole Gunnar Solskjaer commented, "It's perfect for him coming in, we see what he's about. He's about sensing the moment, sensing the danger. He's also evolved into a proper team player. You've got to be there to score the goals and he knows where the goals are scored. There's not many in the world who have scored more than him, so I'm very pleased. But I'm pleased with the whole team and their work rate, we were patient."

Bryan Robson observed that long after the game finished, when fans have normally gone home, they were milling around still savouring the atmosphere. Programmes that are normally left unsold or left behind on tables in lounges were being snapped up just because they marked the day Cristiano returned. "I don't think I've ever seen so many stewards protecting a player when he was doing pitch-side interviews afterwards. Lots of fans had stayed behind hoping to get a glimpse of him or an autograph. It's like a throwback to the glory days, he has given the place new-found belief."

Captain Marvel, as he is still known to fans, felt United didn't give a particularly startling performance but he was sure Ronaldo "will make a difference". Robson had an eye for goal himself as an old fashioned box-to-box midfielder, and he commented; "He senses opportunities, he is clinical, he is a level above. He has the charisma to captivate the crowd and lift them. The level of encouragement being received was that normally afforded for opposition such as Liverpool, Manchester City or Chelsea."

Robson made the point that many of the players back from international duty were off the pace, and that it was a game maybe last year United would have drawn but Ronaldo is always pushing to win. Robson added: "He forced mistakes, anticipated danger and gave United their edge. He and Bruno Fernandes were great at urging their team-mates to pick up the pace and that will rub off on the others."

The margin of victory was harsh on Steve Bruce, as Newcastle actually played well for long periods but Newcastle's efforts were irrelevant to the ecstatic home fans, who had the added bonus of their side returning to the top of the Premier League. Ronaldo proved he still has much to offer at the age of 36, and that the efforts to entice him back to the club were worthwhile. Although he had never previously operated as a striker in the conventional sense, that is where he started - and largely he stayed upfront. He did drop deeper at times, but generally was the most advanced United player.

Ronaldo scored 118 goals in 292 games goals for United between 2003, when he joined as a teenager, and 2009, when he went to Real Madrid for £80m. In the next 12 years he scored 551 goals for Real and Juventus before a surprise £12.8m move back to United on deadline day. His 12 years and 124 days between consecutive Premier League goals is the second-longest behind ex-Everton and Wigan defender Matt Jackson. He is the oldest player to score twice in a Premier League game since Burnley's Graham Alexander in 2010, and the oldest player to score for United in the Premier League since Ryan Giggs in 2013.

United manager Solskjaer played with Ronaldo on his first United debut back in 2003. He was delighted with the Portuguese's return and with the lift it seems to have given the club. United had only won the league title twice since Ronaldo left in 2009 - and have not done so since Sir Alex Ferguson retired in 2013. Their most recent trophy was the 2017 EFL Cup.

"I'm so happy for Cristiano," he told BBC Sport. "I'm so happy for the team and supporters. You sense the atmosphere around the club since he signed. It could easily have been an anti-climax because expectations were so high. It feels like one of the old days. It's special. Cristiano is a special man and a special player for us in the history of the club. He senses big moments and scores goals. He's clinical, he's ruthless. He's lifted the team and everyone around the club. Everyone is dreaming. They can dream and we'll focus."

Solskjaer did not even attempt to disguise his intention to play Ronaldo in the run-up to the game, and asked afterwards whether there was any doubt the Portugal superstar would start, he told Sky Sports: "No, of course not. This is what Man United is about, this is what Cristiano is about and this was a day for everyone to enjoy and they've delivered."

Ronaldo, at 36, may not be the same kind of player while scoring 118 goals during his first spell in England, but a pair of poacher's finishes were a classic hallmark of the new model. "He has developed into a fantastic goalscorer," said Solskjaer, a renowned penalty-box predator himself as a player, "sensing the big moments, knowing where to be, positioning himself in the box, playing a very good game. He drops in, links the play well, but gets in the box when he has to."

Speaking from pitch-side, and struggling to make himself heard over an atmosphere which had been brewing since fans began to gather outside the stadium early in the day, Solskjaer added: "When you win a game, you enjoy it. When you see the fans happy as they are, you really enjoy it and when you see the players coming off, proud of their performance…There were lots of expectations today, for the team, for Cristiano and they delivered. We have to deliver every time. That's Man United - it doesn't change. If you think a few months back, how it was here and now we've got this atmosphere, this is what Man

United supporters should feel like. They should be allowed to dream, but we'll keep our feet on the ground and focus on the next game."

The goals from Ronaldo and Fernandes went some way to answering pre-match questions about whether the two compatriots can gel in the same starting team together. Solskjaer said: "Good players can always play together and they've got such a mutual respect for each other, they play in the national team together. We will work to develop that partnership, of course."

The manager also highlighted Jesse Lingard's contribution - a first United goal since he returned from a loan spell at West Ham, calling it a "fantastic occasion" for the England forward but would not be drawn on the possibility of a Premier League title challenge. "It's too early for me to start predicting where we'll end up," he said. "It's going to be a tight season, we know there's many good teams, but we have to be consistent, keep doing what we do and let's see where we are. When it goes back to one each, you never know how it's going to go. I thought we played well, played the ball and then of course when Luke put on the afterburner and Cristiano of course, he smells the danger. He's so good at timing his runs. You know Bruno, Bruno's quality from those areas. Very, very happy."

As well as Lingard, Donny van de Beek – another midfielder trying to prove himself at United – came on in the second half. "Yeah, I've got to say well done to the club who are bringing in players to challenge and we're bringing competitors. But it's good people and we've built a really strong squad."

Solskjaer was satisfied with the final score in United's first fixture after the September internationals. "You're playing against a team that is well organised, didn't give us loads of space and we had to be patient. It's never easy after an international break to get your tempo and rhythm. We had yesterday to work with everyone together and that was it. I was very pleased with the patience, that we didn't just lose our heads and especially so when they scored in the second-half. We upped the tempo a little bit and we've got quality. So pleased with how efficient we were in front of goal as well."

Greenwood, Edinson Cavani and Anthony Martial are capable of playing through the middle but Ronaldo's goalscoring prowess elevated him to first-choice striker. "He's developed into a miles better footballer than when he was here through the years," Solskjaer said. "Sometimes he can drift off to the sides, turn and finish from there. You're not gonna use him as a battering ram. He likes to roam. The big thing about him is he senses the big moments when to arrive in the box, when to run in behind. I thought he played the game very mature, simple, didn't give too many balls away. I think he gave one ball away, one. But he was very efficient with his football."

Ronaldo played more minutes in the league last season for Juventus than he did in any of his six seasons with United when he was in his teens and early 20s. He scored 29 Serie A goals in 33 games to add to his Premier League (2008) and La Liga (2011, 2014, 2015) golden boots.

Former Newcastle striker Alan Shearer, who was still playing when Ronaldo was at United, was watching the game for Match of the Day said of Ronaldo's performances, "He punished Newcastle. Sometimes you've got to applaud someone. He's been great for such a long time. To come in and do what he has done today - do what he's been doing all his career - is phenomenal. You've got to hold your hands up and have huge respect for him. He keeps on going and going. There doesn't seem to be an end in sight."

Newcastle boss Steve Bruce commented, "That is the goalscoring instinct of a centre-forward, where our defenders haven't followed it in and he is on the end to get a tap in and change the game. If there is a genuine superstar among everyone, then this kid is, with what he has achieved. We have witnessed it again today. He is something else." The magnitude of the occasion did not escape Bruce, who credited his players for making a "big fist" of the game but was in no doubt where the day's story lay. He said: "We're disappointed with the goals we've given away, we've got to be a bit more clinical but we were a threat. We took part in the game and unfortunately weren't good enough."

The joyous occasion was a vivid contrast to the angry scenes at Old Trafford just four months earlier, when the game with Liverpool was postponed amid furious fan protests. There were some chants against the Glazer family and their ownership of the club, but with their team back at the top of the Premier League, Ronaldo's arrival fuelled optimism at levels rarely seen since Sir Alex Ferguson retired in 2013. The absence of live TV coverage meant only those in the ground were witness to the great return, which made even more special for those who were actually there for the Ronaldo Return. 'Come to see United'? 'Come to see Ronaldo' was the chant from the Stretford End.

Eleven days after his scathing assessment of Ronaldo, Paul Merson was back in the Sky Sports studios, this time on Soccer Saturday, covering United's 4-1 win over Newcastle United at Old Trafford on Saturday afternoon. Like pundits do on that show down the years, scream and shout when they are watching a goal, and it was no different for Merson as Ronaldo marked his return to Old Trafford with a bang and Merson with a couple of screams each time he scored. As Ronaldo delivered his trademark celebration in Manchester, Merson, at Sky Studios in London, hailed the five-time Ballon d'Or winner's movement. Considering Merson doubted Ronaldo's movement to a certain level of degree less than a fortnight earlier, the Portuguese ace most certainly proved that he can handle the speed and intensity the Premier League demands, even less than five months away from his 37th birthday.

Merson, who had been critical of the transfer when it went through insisting that United should have signed Harry Kane instead appeared to change his mind after watching the striker against Newcastle describing Ronaldo's movement as "absolutely phenomenal". "The first goal was a mistake by the goalie but there's only one person following up – he's the one who goes 'he's going to spill this' and he taps it in. The second goal, Luke Shaw gets the ball and he sprints. He didn't sprint too many times today – it's a great touch to take it away from [Isaac] Hayden and he hits it hard and low. The goalie will be disappointed – it goes through his legs – but his movement and awareness in seeing it – that's what he's there for." There was still an edge to Merson's observations, as he wasn't backing down completely when he added: "He's not going to close full-backs down, and he played a lot of what I would call wall passes where he just came and kept it ticking over, but his movement was phenomenal. He's not the same player, but if you put the ball in the box or you look up and find time on the ball his movement is absolutely scary. I thought

Cavani's was good, but he is on another planet."

Fans were quick to jump on Merson for his previous comments, suggesting that he didn't know what he was talking about when it came to the player's fitness. But having completed the full 90 minutes with two goals to his name, Ronaldo looked as spritely as ever. Merson was hedging his bets, waiting to see how the season played out however the indicators favoured Ronaldo. Even last season with Juventus, he completed what would equate to 31.1 full 90 minutes across 33 games. Asked about United's chances in the title race Merson stressed that just one game, no matter how well he did, was not going to win the Premier League as he went on, "That's what I said about him when he got more goals than Lukaku last year, but Inter Milan won the league. People said he did his job, but it's a team game. No, your job is to score the goals in the big matches. These ain't going to win you the Premier League these two goals."

Rio Ferdinand felt United should play to one of Ronaldo's greatest strengths and take advantage of a general weakness among Premier League defenders. Ronaldo scored both his goals with his feet, but it is prowess in the air that Rio considered could make a difference as he still retained the ability to defy gravity at times, scoring many times with his head. Rio believed Solskjaer should concentrate on his wingers and overlapping full backs to pick out him out with far more crosses into the box. "One thing from a Man United point of view that they could learn from the weekend's game – and I'm telling you he would have been in there telling them – is just cross that ball when you get the opportunities to cross the ball, you put it in there because he's aggressive and he wants the ball." Rio pointed out that defenders in this country are no longer great at defending crosses, something he had stressed for some tine now. The one time dominating centre half for club and country knew this was an area primed for Ronaldo to exploit due to his extraordinary ability to leap and score with headers as defending headers had become something of a lost art, "When I see balls coming into the box at the moment – the body positions, the angles etc are way off. It ain't easy. I know I've made plenty of mistakes in that position. But I think Ronaldo can exploit some of the naive defending at the moment in the PL."

Ronaldo had now scored 200 braces in professional football for club and country after scoring two in his second debut against Newcastle United at Old Trafford, he was hot property with Newcastle players wanting his shirt. Three Newcastle players were spotted asking for his shirt at full-time. Footage emerged that showed Isaac Hayden, Jamaal Lascelles and Joelinton all wanting Ronaldo's shirt. Each time, Ronaldo turn down their requests suggesting that someone else had already asked him. Maybe he was giving away to someone deserving in the crowd or just wanted to keep it for himself to remind him of his successful United return.

The media had their opinions as well as the pundits….

The Sun: He may now be the wise old head guiding the young guns but Cristiano Ronaldo showed he is ready to do just that after his successful comeback. The returning Manchester United legend also proved he is not just back to help the new generation, he is ready to bring silverware to Old Trafford. Ronaldo grabbed a typical No9's goal with a simple tap-in from three yards out in first half stoppage time for the opener. However, his second was a beauty as he explosively raced onto Luke Shaw's through ball and held off a defender before rifling it straight between keeper Freddie Woodman's legs. It was smiles all-around as the Stretford End sang his name.

Mirror: Even for a man who writes his own scripts, it was quite something. Ronaldo has been and remains an absolute force of nature in the penalty box, and Old Trafford came alive whenever he had the ball anywhere near it early on. His goal on the stroke of half-time was a gift, and one that many a forward would have scored, but he was in the right place at the right time when Woodman did his bit for the narrative.

The Telegraph: At Old Trafford they rose to acclaim a vision of themselves from the past, when a different kind of Manchester United routinely conquered English football, and Europe too, and for an afternoon, at least, Cristiano Ronaldo granted them that privilege. In fact, the reverie lasted so long that it was only the acrimony of the travelling Newcastle United support towards their own club that reminded the home fans to sing that they still wanted the Glazer ownership out – although all that had preceded it had been a thrilling nostalgic journey for them. Ronaldo had returned, 18 years after his first prancing teenage debut, and that alone would have been enough, but the two goals that followed made it a rapturous occasion when United could feel like themselves again. He was received, it would be right to say, like a king. The crowd craning to see him as he came out for the warm-up, the novelty of cheering his name and singing his song seemingly inexhaustible. Up in the stands, Sir Alex Ferguson took his seat in the directors' box.

On Twitter the stars weighed in...

Marcus Rashford MBE 'Like he never left'; Gary

Lineker 'Ronaldouble! What a goalscorer!'

Cristiano Ronaldo's game by numbers vs. Newcastle United: 87% pass accuracy, 8 touches inside the box, 6 shots [5 inside the box], 2 goals, 1.4 xG

8: MUM'S THE WORD

"My mum is the pillar of the family, and what I have today is because she always supported me."

CRISTIANO RONALDO

There was only one way to celebrate. With your mum, of course. Cristiano took his mum Dolores Aveiro out for a meal out on Sunday evening before she returned home. Dolores travelled to the UK to watch her son make his United comeback. The venue for the meal was Piccolino in Hale, Manchester, an up market Italian restaurant chain. Ronaldo has a strict diet which he puts down to maintaining his high fitness levels that have prolonged his career, yet he has one big secret pleasure; he loves pizza. He once said in 2019: "The key is to take care of your body, train, do your recovery and eat properly. Although sometimes I do eat pizza with my son otherwise it would be boring."

Naturally the paparazzi were out in force following Ronaldo's every step, so a night out at a Manchester restaurant was never going to be kept a secret from eager photographers. Delores wore a stylish Louis Vuitton outfit and far from the Ronaldo party being camera shy or worried by the attention, they were used to it as it had been part of their lives for so long. A proud Delores posed for a picture with her son and shared it to her 2.3million followers on Instagram. She wrote: "Good trip, good week to all, kisses!"

It was a rare occasion for Cristiano's 66-year-old mum to watch him in big games because she gets anxious in the stands and has fainted twice with one of her falls breaking her teeth. According to Piers Morgan in the Daily Mail, Ronaldo told him "She's not allowed now to watch big games. I say, 'Listen, I don't have a father any more. I don't want to lose my mum, too, so you're not going to watch quarter finals, semi-finals, or finals." He previously told Morgan: "She gets so nervous, I don't understand why. I get friends to stay with her and she goes for walks around the house. She fainted two times in the stadium. She is nervous."

Ronaldo owes his successful career to her, "My mum is the pillar of the family, and what I have today is because she always supported me. She worked hard to give her best for her children and especially for me because I'm the youngest in the family. She suffered to give me opportunity. I remember when I was 12 and I told her I wanted to go to Lisbon to play with Sporting Lisbon's youth team. She said to me, 'Son, if it's really what you want, I'm not going to cut your legs and stop you. You can go. It will be difficult for me to leave you but go. Follow your dreams.'"

But Piers got it wrong, his mum turned up and was spotted in tears at Old Trafford as she celebrated his remarkable comeback. She also got the chance to spend some time with her grandchildren, posting two pics of her with Cristiano Jr, 11.

After his dream start to his second spell the odds were slashed on Ronaldo becoming the Premier League's leading scorer, joint favourite with Romelu Lukaku and someway ahead of England captain Harry Kane who had fallen to 9/1. Meanwhile United's title odds had also come in to 11/2 while Liverpool's title odds also shortened from to the same price after an impressive 3-0 away win at Leeds United, while Manchester City shifted out slightly to 5-4 from 11-10. Chelsea unchanged at 5-2.

Ronaldo's return raised the expectation levels to land a title for the first time since 2013. There were superior individual performances from him at Old Trafford in his first time at the club, but not for a long time, and never more remarkable than this one given all the circumstances and his age. The expectation was almost overwhelming but Cristiano did what he always does and supporters were left wondering what it means for United's prospects with their team back on top of the table, leading the way in the Premier League. With Ronaldo back, it all felt different, it felt possible, that dreams could come true again in the Theatre of Dreams. The supporters had a reason to believe, with a talisman the envy of their rivals, especially City. Manager Ole Gunnar Solskjaer said: "Handling the pressure is one of the things that you have to do as a Manchester United player, expectations and pressure, you've got to relish it and embrace it and enjoy it — and Cristiano does."

9: THE CHAMPIONS LEAGUE CAMPAIGN

"It's great to have him back, it's massive for us."

DAVID DE GEA

With hype and expectation at an incredible level after just one game, United's manager declined to make any attempt to use the usual football cliches of 'keeping your feet firmly on the ground'. In fact he used the extraordinary degree of anticipation to fuel his team, and indeed, the fans. Ole Gunnar Solskjaer believed he possessed a squad to challenge for the major honours, and that was not based just on the signing of Ronaldo, as there had been other significant acquisitions in the summer transfer window, notably big money signings Raphael Varane and Jadon Sancho but it was the arrival of Cristiano that galvanised everyone inside Old Trafford and made the team one to be feared, as it used to be in the Sir Alex era. That in itself inspired optimism that the club can end a trophy drought that lasted more than four years.

The build up to their first Champions League game of the season at Swiss side Young Boys took on a far different complexion that would have been anticipated when the draw was made. Then, there would have been a united collective shrug of the shoulders from the fan base, no doubt convinced there might be some glory nights, but then there would be an inevitable anti-climax. Suddenly that perception of United changed with the arrival of Ronaldo, and his remarkable Champions league record, having won the precious piece of silverware with 'The Big

Ears' as Ruud Gullit dubbed it, when he was first at the club.

Now the United boss felt it was important to stress that the summer's recruitment was part of a long-term strategy he initially outlined when he took the job just under three years ago, and while Ronaldo was coming toward the end of his illustrious career, the signing of Jadon Sancho was the benchmark for what the manger had in mind about building for the future. "We've had enough disappointments, that's for sure, and some big moments as well," he said. "But this team has grown and matured over the last few seasons. That was always the plan (when I came in), we said in three years' time we'd have a squad with experience and quality that could challenge. With players like David, Harry Maguire, who's been here a couple of years, you get that spine in the team with experience and quality. With Raphael and Cristiano coming in, they add to that. It's not the last bit, you can never say it's the last bit, but it's that something that you have to buy unless you've already won it yourself."

Ronaldo was pictured on social media seated next to Portugal team-mate Diogo Dalot on the private jet. A return to contention for the biggest prizes could also help persuade Paul Pogba, now in the final year of his contract, to re-think his future. "It's up to us to get results and to prove to ourselves that we can win trophies," Solskjaer said when asked about Pogba. "I think everyone that signs for Manchester United wants to win trophies and be part of a winning Manchester United. It's the most magical feeling in the world to be part of a winning Manchester United team."

Solskjaer could finally see the quality required to cope

with the demanding schedule and quantity of competitions throughout his squad. "The players are fitter now and we've been very robust over the years and improved with the way we've dealt with the pandemic and with the games coming thick and fast," he said. "With the ones we've signed it makes it easier to rotate and I've definitely told the team that as well - I do trust all the members of the squad."

Having Ronaldo back was a massive confidence boost, not only among the fans, but also within the dressing room according to goalkeeper David de Gea. After four trophy-less years, Ronaldo was set to make his first Champions League appearance for United since the 2009 final defeat to Barcelona in Rome, with the club back at the top of the Premier League. De Gea was enormously excited by his impact. "It's great to have Cristiano back at home," the goalkeeper said. "I think it shows from the first day when we played at Old Trafford the other day the impact already. He scored two goals, two very important goals for us. You know the qualities but I think the experience of Cristiano is amazing. It's great for us, he's a legend here at the club already. It's great to have him back, it's massive for us."

Solskjaer had to test his man management to the full, to manage Ronaldo's game time, his fitness levels, while the fans wanted him to start every game. The manager said: "Cristiano looks after himself so much so I know he will recover quickly. He has had a pre-season and, of course, it's important that we get everyone up and running and to get him up and running and to give him 90 minutes. It's not impossible to leave him out. He is 36, Mason is 19, so it's the same. I have to manage his minutes, and I have to manage a 36-year-old's minutes as well. Of course there is a game on Tuesday. We will see what we do."

But according to the manager it wasn't only Ronaldo that had the fans believing again, the club has splashed £115.7 million on world class talents Jadon Sancho and Raphael Varane. "I think seeing Raphael and Cristiano coming it's raised everyone's eyebrows because they are winners, they have won everything there is to win and put demands on themselves. The young boys, the rest of the team, they look at them and think that is how you stay at the top."

Ronaldo does not like missing minutes, particularly when he feels there are goals on offer. With Real Madrid leading 2-1 in Levante in February 2018 Zinedine Zidane felt the game was safe enough to take Ronaldo off. The decision backfired as Real drew and Ronaldo kicked off, visibly upset at being withdrawn and he only got angrier as a cameraman zoomed in on his reaction while sat on the bench. Ronaldo told the cameraman: "There is no reason. Look at the game, aim the camera on the game." The Levante match was not the first time Ronaldo's relationship with Zidane had been strained. Sedan substituted Ronaldo at Las Palmas in September 2016 and the forward responded by walking past his manager without even looking at him. Ronaldo sulked on the bench as he watched Las Palmas equalise to draw the match.

During his first season at Juventus Ronaldo responded to being taken off in a home game with AC Milan after just 55 minutes by heading straight down the tunnel after exchanging tense words with Maurizio Sarri. He was replaced by Paulo Dybala who grabbed the winner, but Ronaldo's mood did not change as he left the stadium before the game had even finished. Sarri's successor at Juventus, Andrea Pirlo, also received similar treatment from

Ronaldo, who was hooked when he was on a hat-trick at Inter Milan in February 2012. Juve had fallen behind in a key title clash with Ronaldo striking twice to give his team the lead and ultimately three points, so when Pirlo hauled him off in favour of Alvaro Morata Ronaldo cut a bemused figure as he trudged off the pitch shaking his head before firing a few choice words with his manager.

This was a rare game where Ronaldo missed out altogether, left out for a home game with Roma in August 2020 and he was fuming as he watched from the stands. Still, he had good reason to be cheerful as he collected his second Serie A medal once the match was completed. His chances of winning the golden boot were practically impossible by that stage, as Ciro Immobile scored twice on the final day to finish on 36 goals – five more than Ronaldo. But he would have liked the chance to give it a go in the final game.

Ronaldo taking over as Manchester United manager to replace current boss Ole Gunnar Solskjaer was one of the more outlandish pieces of speculation in the early weeks following his arrival but it certainly got people thinking 'is that possible?', 'is that likely?' And that was the desired effect. With Solskjaer under perpetual pressure after every poor result his job has always been on the line since he succeeded Jose Mourinho in 2018 and Ronaldo didn't help his boss by appearing to coach the side in the closing stages of the defeat to Young Boys in the Champions League.

Former Tottenham manager Tim Sherwood had no issue with Ronaldo being on the touchline alongside his manager shouting instructions, despite suggestions he was undermining Solskjaer. Sherwood even suggest that Ronaldo could replace Solskjaer within 18 months. "I think it's okay that Ronaldo's on the touchline and Ole's going to have to accept it," said Sherwood, speaking to Ladbrokes, "If he brings him to his football club you've got to know what you're bringing in. It's a completely different Ronaldo to the one who was at Old Trafford the first time around. He knows how he's needed and if he feels like he needs to stand next to the manager and give instructions then you've got to let him do that."

Mind you, Sherwood didn't think that would have happened with someone like Jose Mourinho in charge, a vastly more experience coach wouldn't stand for it! Sherwood also wondered why Ronaldo felt it necessary to stand up and give some instruction in the first place. Sherwood commented: "We've seen him do it on the international stage, most recently at the Euros, barking out orders. That boy will be a manager 100 per cent. I would have a bet on him being Manchester United manager in 18 months. Whenever Ronaldo finishes playing I think he will become a manager, it will be an automatic choice. If they win the Premier League, Champions League, FA Cup, any of those trophies, then Solskjaer keeps his job, but if they don't win anything I think they've got a manager there in the making."

Sherwood argued that Ronaldo would be an instant hit as a manager especially if he brought in an experienced coach to work with him, such as Carlos Queiroz, "He's almost coaching now - you saw it at the weekend during the warm-up whispering in Varane's and Maguire's ears, but I don't think it's that he needs the captain's armband to be a leader, he leads by example anyway. He did when he was at United the first time it's just now he's being more vocal with it."

10: THE GREATEST EVER?

*'From all the records that I have broken during my career – and
fortunately there have been a few – this one is very special for me
and it's certainly on the shelf of the achievements that make me
truly proud.'*

CRISTIANO RONALDO

Cristiano Ronaldo made his Champions League
debut for Manchester United in 2003, but his first
appearance on the continent was a 2-1 upset in
Stuttgart after Sir Alex's team conceding two goals in two
minutes. Ruud van Nistelrooy's penalty was only a late
consolation. The infamous Fergie 'hairdryer' was aimed at
his entire team after the match, criticising their defending
and lack of patience, if indeed, the players could take in what
he was shouting and screaming at them! "We defended
terribly for the two goals and if you defend badly in games
of this nature you deserve everything that happens to
you," explained Fergie to the media when he had cooled
down. "From a position of control we surrendered within
minutes, and allowed Stuttgart to become strong. We
committed ourselves to winning balls we shouldn't have
been winning, all we needed to do was drop off to the edge
of the box and be patient."

However, Ronaldo had a reasonably good game under
the circumstances on the night and won the penalty for
Van Nistelrooy, however, Stuttgart coach Felix Magath
insisted the Portuguese's theatrics did not warrant a spot
kick, which was a sign of much controversy to come over

Ronaldo's ability to win penalties, with ensuing accusation of diving. "I think the actions of our goalkeeper were absolutely correct," said Magath after Timo Hildebrand was punished for tripping Ronaldo. "He was going for the ball and he used his hands so there was no reason to give a penalty."

Remarkably Ronaldo failed to score during his debut Champions League campaign for United, but he left the club in 2009 with16 Champions League goals, his best season was the triumphant 2007/08 campaign, scoring eight including the opener in the final in Moscow, and went on to become the greatest every Champions league goalscorer. Given his current insane statistics it is astonishing, therefore, and considering Ronaldo's remarkable greatness in this competition, that it took him until his fourth season at United to score in the Champions League proper but it was worth waiting for, as it was some goal by which but to break your duck. And it was a memorable night in 2007 as United crushed AS Roma 7-1 with Ronaldo with a brilliant brace, the first goal of which was a very classy strike, and his all round game was sublime as United progressed into the semi-finals. 2007 was his breakout season at United, with more than 20 goals for the first time in his career. Ronaldo has gone on to add 133 more since that brace against Roma, and was the leading goalscorer in the competition's history and added another in his first game back in the Champions league in a United shirt.

The 2008 Champions League Final was one to savour and packed with drama. He scored a glorious header, only to almost cost United by missing in the shootout but his performance was a mouth watering combination of glorious close control, mesmerising step overs and was easily the man of the match against Chelsea. Ronaldo won his first ever Champions League trophy as United defeated Chelsea on penalties.

Frank Lampard cancelled out his header to send the game the full distance. When the match went to penalties and Ronaldo missed his penalty, he was spared any potential embarrassment as John Terry slipped and missed what would've been the winning penalty for Chelsea when he struck the outside of the post. Edwin van der Sar saved Nicolas Anelka's spot kick, as United were crowned European champions.

When it comes to spectacular goals Ronaldo loves to bask in the glory of creating something quite beautiful, an art form, and he pulled off some wonderful strikes during his United early days when he became the first ever recipient of the Puskas Award. Ronaldo achieved the accolade on the Champions League stage, with a glorious strike into the top corner past Helton in the Porto goal from fully 40 yards to help his side reach the Champions League semi-finals, all the sweeter scoring against the Portuguese side. Ronaldo joined United from Sporting Lisbon, who had a long-standing rivalry with Porto, and the Portuguese takes extra pride in scoring against his former rivals. Ronaldo has scored against them in the Champions League for United, Madrid and Juventus. He then bagged a brace at the Emirates in the semi-final when he baffled everybody to score a free-kick from 40 yards with commentator Clive Tyldesley saying just before he struck the wonder free-kick: "Too far for Ronaldo to think about it." There can't be too many better ways than scoring a brace to book your sides place in the Champions League final that this performance against Arsenal at the Emirates

Stadium during a semi-final second leg in 2009, as his side made it to the final for the second successive year. Both goals were different, one was that outrageous free-kick, the other was a blistering counter-attack, with Ronaldo starting the move before sprinting the entire length of the field to score as he stretched Arsene Wenger's side.

When Real Madrid beat rivals Atletico in 2014 to seal "La Decima" – their 10th European title. Ronaldo struck a 120th minute penalty. The last minute strike was his 17th goal of the competition that season, an incredible tally that is still a Champions League record and one never likely to be equalled with a staggering nine goals in the group stages, seven in the knockout rounds and finishing with the fourth goal in the final against Atletico Madrid. Ronaldo personifies calm under pressure and walking from the half-time to take a Champions League deciding penalty is the ultimate nerve-tester. Ronaldo showed nerves of steel to once again dish out heartbreak for Atletico in the final.

Ronaldo notched two goals at the Allianz Arena and then a hat-trick at Old Trafford, one of Ronaldo's greatest Champions League performances over two legs, as Madrid beat Bayern Munich 6-3 on aggregate in 2016/17. Ronaldo's incredible five goals during their quarter final success against the Bundesliga giants enabled Madrid to progress to win the Champions League again. Ronaldo scored his 100th European goal in the first leg against Bayern, becoming the first player in history to reach a century in just 143 appearances, scoring his second 50 goals in a mere 47 games.

Ronaldo's greatest Champions League goal was his overhead kick in 2018 at Juventus, which was even applauded by the home crowd, who became very familiar with Ronaldo shortly after. Madrid beat Juventus 3-0 that night in the first leg of their quarter final. He was again the hero in the second leg, scoring a last minute penalty to send his side through. Ronaldo then joined Juventus that summer for 100m (£88m).

The first time Ronaldo had to perform a major rescue mission in the Champions League came in 2015/16 after a 2-0 first-leg defeat to Wolfsburg. He levelled the scores in 84 first-half seconds before completing the turnaround with a trademark free-kick but he took the comeback to a different level with Juve against tough defending Atletico Madrid. Ronaldo levelled the scores with two all-conquering headers for the Turin side completing his hat-trick from the penalty spot.

Ronaldo was signed by Juventus to try and lead them to Champions League success, and he pulled off a marvellous performance against former Madrid rivals Atletico. Diego Simeone's side thought they had seen the back of Ronaldo as he departed La Liga, but they were drawn against Juve in the round of 16 the following season. Even at 34 Ronaldo stunned Atleti as he scored a hat-trick in the second leg to overturn a 2-0 deficit and knock out Simeone's side. He explained following the final whistle: "This was why Juventus brought me here".

Ronaldo likes nothing better than to break records, some of which will never be equalled. He matched Iker Casillas' Champions League appearance record in the first group stage game against Swiss side Young Boys. It marked his 177th Champions League appearance - equalling the record held by Real Madrid legend. He has already became the all-time top international scorer when he powered superb headers in the 89th and 96th minutes against the

Republic of Ireland to beat Ali Daei's 109-goal record and move onto 111. For 89 minutes it was all going wrong with a missed penalty and a scuffle with Dara O'Shea that could have led to a red card. Portugal peppered the Irish goal with 29 shots, Ronaldo himself fired in eight. Then, in the 89th-minute, Goncalo Guedes' cross was headed home by the veteran to break Daei's record. With virtually the last kick of the tie he grabbed the winner. Mario provided the ball in and once again Ronaldo guided his header home. He whipped off his shirt in trademark fashion as Estadio Algarve wildly celebrated as he held his iconic No7 jersey aloft. On full-time he took away both match balls he scored with as an extra trophy. A yellow card for his celebration meant he headed to Manchester rather than to Azerbaijan for the friendly with Qatar. He declared after the final whistle: "I'm happy not only because I got the record but for the special moments that we had with two goals at the end. I have to appreciate what the team did. We believed until the end. For the supporters, I'm so happy." On the penalty miss, Ronaldo added: "It's part of the game. Sometimes we score, sometimes you [make a] mistake. It's part of the business. But I still believed until the end of the game so I am so glad to score and win the game."

11: RONALDO SCORES AGAIN

"Cristiano's exceptional but we have to look after him and it felt like the right moment to take him off."

OLE GUNNAR SOLSKJAER

Ole Gunnar Solskjaer indicated he would manage Ronaldo's minutes in his advancing years, but by starting him against Young Boys, it sent a clear message that United and Ronaldo were eager to bring the Champions League back to Old Trafford in 2022. The Champions League campaign began in Switzerland with two players who had each won the competition four times with Real Madrid, including La Decima - Madrid's 10th triumph in the European Cup - followed by three more Champions Leagues in the four seasons. Optimism was high, expectation soaring. Could United win the coveted Champions league again with such vast experience recruited to their ranks.

Solskjaer thought so. He knew the spine of the team was finally in place, with the experience and quality. Solskjaer observed: 'Of course, with Raphael and Cristiano coming in, they add that last… not last bit, you can never say it's the last bit. It's something extra we have to buy unless you win it four times yourself. That was always the plan when I came in, that we had a squad with experience and quality to challenge. The atmosphere is really good and that's definitely going to stand us in good stead. It's great to have Cristiano back at home. The impact showed on the first day we played, with two very important goals for us. You know the qualities, the experience of Cristiano is amazing. It's massive for us. He's a legend here and it's great to have him back. It's up to us now to get results and prove to ourselves we can win trophies.'

The warm up was bizarre enough, and the match itself was a total anti-climax as United shot themselves in the foot. Ronaldo accidentally KO'd a match steward while warming up when he fired a ball wide of the goal as he limbered up and hit a steward standing on the sideline. The fierce impact saw the woman crash to the ground. People quickly looked to make sure she was okay and Ronaldo immediately went over to check on her. After knowing the steward was ok, Ronaldo ran back onto the pitch to continue his warm-up.

The incident didn't put him off as he became the first player to score the first Champions League goal in two different seasons when he opened United's account after just 13 minutes. The gap 4,515 days between his last European goal for United and this one - against Arsenal in May 2009. He scored for the 16th straight season in the Champions League. He shares that distinction with Messi and Benzema but Messi was likely to jump ahead once he scored with his new club Paris St Germain.

A fabulous ball with the outside of his foot by Fernandes from the left carved open the Young Boys defence and Ronaldo was left with a tap in which once more squirmed through the keeper's legs. That was Ronaldo's sixth touch of the game, fewer than any United outfield player. However a red card for Aaron Wan-Bissaka proved pivotal. A reorganised United team attempted to hold on for the in the second half but Moumi Ngamaleu levelled and before a Jesse Lingard backpass fell for Siebatcheu who struck in injury time to win the game for the Swiss. United didn't have a single shot on or off target after the 25th minute and only saw 30.7% possession in the second half. United equalled their club Champions League record of three consecutive defeats, set from December 2004 to March 2005.

At the final whistle Ronaldo made the female steward smile by presenting her with his No 7 shirt. Marisa Nobile said later that she thought she was dead before the Portuguese superstar told her otherwise after an apologetic Ronaldo jumped over the barrier to check on the welfare of the stricken steward as she received medical attention. Nobile initially feared the worst before those concerns were allayed by the iconic No 7. 'When the ball hit me on my head it was a full strike!' she told Blick TV. 'I was gone in my head and went to the ground. Afterwards I saw Ronaldo above me! Me: "Oh my god no, did I die?" 'Ronaldo said: "No, no. Excuse me! What's happening? Are you all right?" 'I was in great pain. My God. I was more or less but then I saw Ronaldo and the headache was gone.'

Having missed out on qualifying for the knockout stages last season, United would face Villarreal in their next Group F game at Old Trafford in a repeat of last season's Europa League final.

Solskjaer commented, "That is football for you at the highest level. A lack of concentration, make a mistake and you get punished. We did that last year in Europe, we conceded two sloppy counter attacks against Basaksehir. Today in the last seconds Jesse wants to play it safe and one misplaced pass and you concede a goal. If Jesse gets that chance again he would swivel and clear it but we will learn from it."

Ronaldo was surprisingly subbed along with Bruno Fernandes with 18 minutes remaining and the score at 1-1. The manager blamed the tiring effect of the Astroturf for taking off Ronaldo and bringing on Matic for his experience and for Lingard's freshness, but it all went wrong in every sense. "Cristiano is exceptional but we have to look after him and it felt like the right moment to take him off," explained Solskjaer.

Fans were not impressed however and felt the decision was 'bizarre' to swap the striker and play the midfielder as a false nine. Jadon Sancho was also hauled off, before Donny van de Beek was subbed at the break as Solskjaer went for a 5-3-1. Another issue revolving around Ronaldo. Who else? A throw back to his first United phase when he was the centre of much controversy over diving for penalties. The incident in question materialised when United were 1-0 up. The 32-year-old French referee Francois Letexier waved away Ronaldo's appeal after he was bundled over in the box by keeper Mohamed Ali Camara. Solskjaer's take on it was that the young ref should also have handed out a red card, so backed away from the double whammy. The manager pointed out that the keeper shoved over Ronaldo with his arm in a one-on-one situation.

Solskjaer put a consoling arm around Ronaldo when he hauled him off, no doubt sympathetic that he should have had a penalty, and the manager felt he was justified in his decision to make that substitution as it was "the right moment" and he was conscious of managing his game time, but the fan base was hugely critical of taking off a proven goalscorer just when you need a goal.

What happened next added to the drama and controversy surrounding Ronaldo, and inspired even greater debate.

Ronaldo was animated on the touchline after he had been taken off, something that pundits didn't approve of, but something the passionate competitor did for his country to great effect, almost becoming one of the coaches, and certainly aiming to motivate his players still on the pitch. Ronaldo was famously vocal during Portugal's Euro 2016 final victory after being stretchered off!

Rio Ferdinand, a lead pundit for Champions League broadcaster BT Sport, felt Solskjaer should have told Ronaldo to sit down on the touchline. Speaking after the game on BT Sport, Ferdinand said: "If I'm the manager, I've got to be honest, I'm telling him to sit down." Fellow pundit Peter Crouch backed Rio but recognised Ronaldo's reputation brings certain privileges. He said: "If I'm sitting on the bench as well I'm telling him to sit down. But he is Cristiano, we'll let him do it."

Paul Scholes believed Solskjaer's tactics did not help United. Lingard was the third substitution of five made by Solskjaer on the night. Sancho came off for Diogo Dalot following Wan-Bissaka's red. Varane replaced Donny van de Beek, while Nemanja Matic and Anthony Martial came on later on. According to Scholes, though, Solskjaer should have brought Martial into the game earlier than the 89th minute. While a win or even a draw would have been acceptable, defeat was not viewed as a complete disaster by Scholes, who knew this was actually one of the weakest groups. The pundit told BT Sport that while Lingard would be distraught with his error right at the end, the defeat all stemmed from the sending off in the first half. United were quite comfortable up until that point, Scholes thought. "I do think United probably missed a trick, they couldn't get out their half they were so deep. I think he should've brought more pace on earlier in Martial or Greenwood, they didn't do that and they've paid the ultimate price."

This was not United's first experience of this kind of shock set back in their recent European memory, though. They lost in a similar fashion to Istanbul Basaksehir in the Champions League last season with Demba Ba's bizarre breakaway goal and then lost 2-1. "It's Basaksheir all over again. We were here last season and rueing mistakes," Rio Ferdinand said. "That's a big mistake at the end of the game from Jesse who done really well at the weekend. [It] just goes to show wherever you go in Europe it's tough. You have to be on your game. You have to be mentally tuned in. Yeah, they started well and a decision in the game can change it. It was a bad touch, a bad tackle then the game turned on its head totally."

Peter Schmeichel joined a growing group of ex-United players to express their criticisms of the manager's handling of what the former goalkeeper described as 'strange' tactics in their 2-1 loss to Young Boys. Solskjaer had now lost seven of 11 Champions League matches as United boss and Schmeichel was one of many observers to question the Norwegian's thinking against Young Boys and indeed other ties. The bookies had already slashed the odds on Ole getting sacked!

Solskjaer may have had one eye on the club's weekend Premier League fixture against West Ham, which influenced his selection with Raphael Varane not starting the match, but Schmeichel felt the manager should have selected his strongest team, as the trip to east London wasn't until the Sunday, with plenty of recovery time. Schmeichel made his observations in an interview with CBS Sports where he was irritated by a profusion of excuses from the United manager, including his post-match complaints about the artificial pitch at Young Boys stadium, Schmeichel felt that regardless of Astroturf, whatever excuses you come up with, get that win in the opening group game, where the opposition was hardly formidable to say the least.

Mason Greenwood was in great form, creating chances and taking his own chances, and Schmeichel was surprised he was left out. He was particularly confused with Solskjaer's decision to take off Ronaldo, pointing out that he could have been the difference in the tie. The United legend was also baffled at replacing the Portuguese forward with Jesse Lingard. Talking as a fan, Schmeichel said the fans want Ronaldo on the pitch, regardless of if they're down to 10 men, because if he gets the ball he can make something happen. "The supporters have been crying out for a very long time to have that kind of player. Yet, the manager sends on a player he clearly doesn't trust as he put him out on loan to West Ham, and somebody he desperately tried to sell. I just find it strange." Solskjaer's decision to bring on Anthony Martial when United were seeking to close out the game was another baffling move for Schmeichel to try to get his head around, as he said that was "really weird because Martial doesn't defend well, he doesn't work hard, he's a goalscorer but we're down to 10 men, we don't expect to create many chances, so why put Martial on?'

Ronaldo was upbeat despite the defeat tweeting "Wasn't the result we wanted, but now it's time to recover well and focus on the next game!"

12: TIME TO DELIVER THE TITLE

As the Ronaldo Roadshow headed to east London Ole Gunnar Solskjaer found himself having to defend himself against accusations he allowed Cristiano Ronaldo to 'coach' on the touchline after the manager had substituted him in the midweek Champions League tie. The United manager pointed out that the rules only allow for one man in the technical area and that's either the manager or one of the coaches: Michael Carrick, Mick Phelan or Kieran McKenna. When Ronaldo and Fernandes leapt up and ended up in the technical area, Ole said: It was just spur of the moment, he should have been sent off, so I don't have any problem with them showing some passion and then going back down. It's not like he [Ronaldo] was coaching the players, no."

Solskjaer also felt it necessary to address an abundance of opinions from the pundits that Ronaldo's arrival would restrict the development of young players such as Mason Greenwood with the manager making it clear that he has not had to change anything to accommodate one of football's biggest legends and that Ronaldo has been a team player, not a diva. "All new players, you manage the training sessions because they have to get used to the way we do things. But Cristiano has been here before, he knows how we do things and we have not really had to adapt any training at all. Tactically he gets what we want from him. It is about getting the best out of the team, not one player. You can say you want the best out of Bruno, you want the best out of Mason, you want the best out of Jadon [Sancho] or Anthony [Martial]."

The manager has a big squad now and with so many players his mantra is that is "we work together as a team". He explained: "The stronger the collective, the more chance for an individual to get goals or assists, then we celebrate together. Cristiano has come exactly as we hoped. He knows Man United, he's been here before, the same with Tom Heaton who has also come back. The two of them know the culture, they know what we do, they've learnt it here. They've given these young boys at the club glimpses of what you can have in your career."

Making his name at Burnley and earning three England caps, Heaton moved to Villa before an injury cut his spell there short - and the 35-year-old returned to United. He praised Ronaldo for setting the marker for how the rest of the United squad should train. "I saw first-hand the work ethic and the desire and the drive that went into his journey to doing what he's done. You know, we're certainly seeing that same sort of desire and drive around the training ground in the first few days. Everyone in the building can take something from that. He's the marker, the pinnacle of where everyone wants to be at. It's a brilliant addition obviously on the pitch but also behind the scenes.'

Ole said that the senior players such as Ronaldo talk to the younger ones about their own previous experiences. Solskjaer went on, "How we do things here is within the walls and you have to experience it to be able to pass it on. Anthony Elanga, Mason, Marcus for that matter, Anthony Martial as well. They are still young players and can learn off the best. They know the expectations and the circus and everything that happened before the Newcastle game, Cristiano handled it well and the other players handled it well. It's what we do. Good players come in and you learn from them but you still want to take their place.'

Solskjaer did not mind fans dreaming of a first Premier League title win since Sir Alex retired in 2013, as long everyone remains focused and not get carried away by believing that those expectations will simply turn up and win - he was demanding hard work and application, a message Ronaldo was supporting, in order to achieve their ambitions. "That's why you're here, at the biggest club in the world," said Solskjaer. "It is called the Theatre of Dreams for a reason because, if you [the fans] don't dream high, what are you there to support your team for? That's for the supporters. I'm grounded, the coaches are grounded. We know our expectations. We know we have good players. But we also know we're in a competitive situation where every single game and every single training session counts and we can't take our eye off the ball and dream."

Manchester City had already dropped five points, losing to Spurs on the opening weekend and drawing at home to Southampton the day before United played at West Ham. City were second, three points behind Liverpool who had maintained their unbeaten start to the season with a 3-0 win against Palace. United and fourth-placed Chelsea could move above City and level with Liverpool when they faced West Ham and Tottenham. Pundits were already suggesting that City, Chelsea, United and Liverpool made up a four-way race for the title but Graeme Souness believes there were more question marks over United than the other title contenders. "United have not won any major trophies recently and have spent a great deal of money. Liverpool and City have been the real deal for the past few years and Chelsea have won the Champions League. If you put it like that, it's common sense. The other ones have not only won trophies, but the big trophies, the important ones."

While conceding that Solskjaer had brought in world class players Souness refused to put United in the same category as their rivals because of their recent trophy drought. "I agree this is the strongest top four we've seen in the Premier League for several years," Souness said in his Sunday Times column.

Fabinho rated City and Chelsea as Liverpool's two biggest title rivals with City as favourites "as they're the defending champions and still keep strengthening themselves, which is what they do every season. They, even being champions, always want to reinforce, so they are favourites for the season. Chelsea, current Champions League champions, keep buying, too. I think these two teams come really strong, too, and are the favourites.'

Paul Scholes warned Solskjaer that he simply had to deliver a major trophy for Manchester United this season, preferably their first Premier League title since 2013 after they finished second and without any silverware last season. With big money buys Jadon Sancho, Raphael Varane and Cristiano Ronaldo the Red Devils had a good platform, winning three of their four opening games in the Premier League to leave them leading the table but they urgently needed to put that demoralising 2-1 defeat to Young Boys in their group-stage opener behind them, and Ronaldo would be a calming influence within the dressing room, motivating the players to get back on track immediately at West Ham, and their former United manager David Moyes.

Scholes stressed that after two years of the current management regime it was time to deliver on the back on strengthening the spine of the team with world class players. While United's playing strength now made them contenders on every level with the best in the Premier League, it might not be the same by the quality of the manger. United's rivals all possessed manager who had proven track records as winners at the very highest level, but not so United. Scholes praised Solskjaer for doing "a fantastic job to build this squad" but said that "Now is the time.You look at the team sheet, you look at the bench… he has to win something with this team this season."

Former Old Trafford and Northern Ireland goalkeeper Roy Carroll believed that he knew his one time United team-mate Ronaldo well enough to know that even at the age of 36 he wasn't back at United for a lap of honour to celebrate a spectacular career and will be as driven as he was first time around to win trophies. After a gap of 26 years without the title, until United won the league in 1993, Fergie's signing of Eric Cantona from Leeds, inspired the revival, and the can now happen with Ronaldo. City, Chelsea, Leicester and Liverpool had all been champions since Fergie's final glory run. When David Beckham left for Real Madrid in 2003, Carroll thought he would be able to take a break from facing endless free-kicks after training. Then Cristiano came along and the set-piece practice routines became more intense.

Jamie Carragher's concern was that Ronaldo would cause 'as many problems as it solves' for the manager in his column for The Telegraph, where he questioned whether Ronaldo's arrival gets them any closer to challenging for their first title since 2013. He argued that "for all the understandable euphoria… his signing causes as many problems as it solves for Ole Gunnar Solskjaer." He thought that Ronaldo's return to English football was more beneficial for the Premier League as a whole than for Manchester United as the club who brought him back to these shores. "The broader question for United is whether Ronaldo's arrival gets them any nearer to being a team that can win the title and Champions League again. On the evidence of the first few games, albeit they have won three of their first five matches, I would say no. Ronaldo's match-winning ability will inevitably make United stronger. What his arrival alone cannot do is turn United into a title-winning unit or impose the distinctive way of playing they still lack."

Carragher compared Manchester United to their other likely challengers City, Chelsea and Liverpool where all of United's' rivals possessed 'identifiable and settled style, but by comparison Manchester United are a team of brilliant individuals who need to be 'moulded into a collective force'. Carragher believed Ronaldo could have an impact on Sancho's place in the team, "The most immediate impact is on Sancho, who is now fighting with Greenwood for his favoured position on the right. He played on the left wing in his first two United appearances, switching flanks in midweek prior to being subbed early when the team was reduced to 10 men. There are also consequences for Pogba. After his encouraging start, he was back in centre-midfield against Wolverhampton Wanderers, Newcastle and for the last hour in midweek, when we saw the same flaws that have typified his United career. Where will Marcus Rashford fit into the equation upon his return from injury? And then there is Edinson Cavani, who Solskjaer was talking up in his latest press conference. It sounds like the manager does not want any of his stars to feel like they are back-ups."

Gary Neville had expressed similar views immediately

after Ronaldo signed when he told Sky Sports News, "The big question every Manchester United fan, probably every fan in the Premier League, will be asking will be: is it enough for them to challenge for the title and win the title? I don't quite feel it is. I still feel there are a couple of teams that are better. The Premier League I think is the strongest it's been since the mid-2000s."

Former United midfielder Jose Kleberson joined a growing group of ex players convinced the Reds were the favourites to win the title with the arrival of Ronaldo and key signings. United were joint top on 10 points after four games alongside Chelsea, Liverpool and Everton. Jose argued: "That's just because of the signing of Ronaldo alongside existing players like Paul Pogba and Bruno Fernandes. Those guys a very powerful in an attacking sense, however, Chelsea have a great manager." He felt Chelsea would be the main contenders due to the way Thomas Tuchel makes his teams very organised and is great at prioritising the team over the players and he was expecting a great game when Chelsea played United.

Ed Woodward believed the club were on track to win silverware after a strong summer of recruitment ass the club announced their latest financial figures. Outgoing executive vice-chairman Woodward said tangible progress was being made under Ole Gunnar Solskjaer to enable United to challenge for major honours. Woodward said the summer signings of £135million were possible by the club's commercial strength which also helped ward off the impact of the pandemic. He said it has been an exciting start to the season at Old Trafford, with capacity crowds in attendance for the first time in almost 18 months. The club were delighted to welcome back Cristiano Ronaldo, along with marquee signings of Raphael Varane and Jadon Sancho plus the arrival of Tom Heaton, "to further reinforce the progress that our first team has been making under Ole".

Behind the scenes the commercial power of Gold Trafford continued to power forward made possible by the strength of the clubs operating model, with sustained investment in the team "underpinned by robust commercial revenues". Woodward commented: "Everyone associated with Manchester United can be proud of the resilience we have shown through the challenges created by the pandemic and we look forward to the rest of the season and beyond with great optimism."

United recorded an operating loss of £36.9million last season due to the impact of Covid-19. In their previous annual results, revenue dropped from £627.1m to £509m - figures that incorporated just a three-month hit of the coronavirus pandemic. The economic ramifications continued in the year ending June 30, 2021, with United seeing revenue drop down to £494.1m. The net loss of £92.2m - up 297.4 per cent from £23.2m in 2020 - was largely down to the accounting impact of a £66.6m non-cash tax charge. Net debt was down from £474.1m to £419.5m year on year, thanks in no small part to season ticket revenues and favourable exchange rate. Champions League participation was a key reason behind wages increasing by 13.6 per cent to £322.6m.

Speaking to investors on a conference call, Woodward added, "We have been clear in our strategy to build a squad with a blend of top-class recruits and home-grown talent, comprising a balance of youth and experience, with the aim of winning trophies and playing attacking football the Manchester United way. As part of this, we have continued to strengthen our recruitment and scouting processes, and we have also increased our investment in the Academy, to ensure that this success is sustainable. While squad-building is a constant process, we are more confident than ever that we are on the right track. It is not an accident that we have been able to invest this summer at a time when many clubs have been retrenching. This reflects the strong commercial model we have built over many years, ensuring that our spending is always underpinned by revenues that we generate ourselves.

However, while we are confident in our relative strength, it remains clear that football as a whole faces major financial challenges caused by years of material inflation in wages and transfer fees, exacerbated by the impact of the pandemic."

United were among a dozen clubs from England, Spain and Italy that tried to break away and form a European Super League earlier this year. This led to furious fan protests and a U-turn inside 48 hours and Woodward acknowledged the strength of feeling, "While we are confident in our relative strength, it remains clear that football as a whole faces major financial challenges caused by years of material inflation in wages and transfer fees, exacerbated by the impact of the pandemic. We are committed to working within the Premier League, the ECA and UEFA to promote greater financial sustainability at all levels of the game. We want to be part of healthy, vibrant domestic and European football pyramids, working together with our governing bodies and, most importantly, the fans, to preserve and enhance the magic of our game."

United's wage bill was expected to leap by a fifth to eclipse the British record of £387million. City reported record salaries of £351m in their latest set of figures, accounting for the 2019-20 season. United's chief financial officer Cliff Baty forecast the club's wages for last season, which was below City and increased to £322m by virtue of Champions League qualification, will go up by 'around 20 per cent' inflated by the summer recruitment of Cristiano Ronaldo, Raphael Varane and Jadon Sancho, increasing the total by £64m. "In terms of costs, we'd expect wages to increase by around 20 per cent which reflects the increased investment in the squad following the summer transfer window," Baty said as United released their annual accounts.

City, United and Liverpool were the top three spenders on salaries, and the Old Trafford faithful want to see those balance sheets turned into team sheets they can rely on to bring the big prizes back to the club. The fans delight and excitement at seeing Ronaldo back at United was relentless, and although one of football's first billionaires, he retained his down to earth approach, stopping in his car on way to training when he caught sight of a homemade sign outside the entrance to the Carrington complex. His message written across a piece of cardboard: 'Ronaldo, please could you stop? It would make my weekend.' Ronaldo briefly pulled over for United fan Callum and took a picture. The veteran was the first United player to report for training the day before their clash with West Ham, yet again setting an example to the rest of the squad.

It would be a testing time at the Hammers where David Moyes had build an exciting and potentially successful team. Solskjaer in particular would be tested, his credentials to be the manager to lead the team to a title challenge. The manager observed that his side's recent success in a blistering start to the Premier League campaign was purely to a desire to get on the ball and win the game. Solskjaer replied when asked about players doing several roles: "Overarching philosophy? I don't sit here and claim that. Football is a simple game, it's about making good decisions, it's about your qualities, it's about being in a team and sometimes we look too much into the little intricacies. It's passion, it's desire, it's who wants to win that tackle, who wants to win that ball, which one of the strikers has got the desire to get on the end of crosses."

Solskjaer wanted winners, and he had plenty now in his dressing room, none more so than Ronaldo, which made him feel he was "getting there with my team" because they were not simply brilliant individuals but also team players. With three goals in two games the manager was expecting Ronaldo to continue to show his world–class ability in front of goal. "Yes, you know, it's about his longevity and sustainability and his professionalism and his quality. He scored again and I'm sure he'll score more goals for us."

Solskjaer felt that Ronaldo and the rest of his squad handled the intense scrutiny of Ronaldo's' return against Newcastle and that impressed him. He faced the Hammers twice in the space of four days, with a Carabao Cup third–round tie at Old Trafford following hot on the heels of the league clash, and it was clear the manager was thinking of resting Ronaldo for the cup tie and bringing Edinson Cavani back from injury in a perfect low key tie when both team were bound to show multiple changes.

Solskjaer was "doing a really good job" and had all the ingredients to lead United to the title according to Hammers boss David Moyes. The Scot knew from experience that United will always have to be competitive and try to win trophies, especially the title something it was renowned for in the past, but not in recent times. Moyes managed the Red Devils for 10 months between 2013 and 2014 and was quickly dismissed for failing to get the club back on track. Now he argued they have a good balance of youth and experience in the squad. He said: "I think Ole's been given a really good chance to build a squad and a team and I think he's doing a good job. He's got a team that is more than capable this year of winning the Premier League."

Roy Keane was critical of the club's early-season away form but backed Solskjaer's side to bounce back from their humiliating defeat at BSC Young Boys. Speaking to Sky Sports, Keane wasn't shocked by United's defeat in their Champions League opener. Despite the unbeaten start to the Premier League, Keane remained unconvinced by their performances on the road. He said: "The signs haven't been great the last few weeks away from home. I think away from home against Southampton, they weren't great and could have lost that. At Wolves, they did get the win, and their performance wasn't great, so I wasn't that shocked [with the loss to Young Boys]. It was a poor error at the end of the game from Jesse, but I did see it coming. They'll bounce back. Everything is exaggerated at United. They beat Newcastle, and everything is great; they lose during the week, it's a disaster. It's still early in the season. They've got three or four new faces into the club; it takes time to bed in. They'll be disappointed with the defeat but they'll bounce back."

It seemed that so much was riding on the golden touch of Ronaldo, but Ole had to carry the entire team with him to get the best of out such a prolific goalscorer and serial winner. Solskjaer recognised that he had to leave a legacy of winning silverware at Old Trafford with mounting pressure to win his first trophy as United manager since being appointed in March 2019. A winner of six Premier League titles, two FA Cups and a Champions League as a United player, he came agonisingly close to lifting the Europa League in last year's campaign, only to be denied on penalties by Villarreal. "Yeah of course [the fans are desperate for silverware] that's the ultimate aim, that's what we are here for, that's the history that we have and that's the legacy that we have to leave behind whenever we leave at the end. That's the focus, that's the aim, that's the ambition, to get to April or May in that position [near the top of the table], though you have to stay calm, keep doing what you do and work well in training. Of course we sense the expectations on us this season, we sensed the circus around the Newcastle game. Everyone in Manchester, they have an opinion on football now, which is great, and that's what we want at Man Utd – we want that buzz."

Solskjaer anticipated a tough battle even though the Hammers were without Antonio, this season's Premier League top scorer, due to suspension. "They're a very good side, but every side you play against in the Premier League has dangers and individual players who can hurt you." said the United boss.

While everyone was talking 'Ronaldo', Solskjaer backed Sancho to settle in the Premier League and become a key player at Old Trafford for the next "10 or 12 years". The United manager appreciated that the arrivals of Ronaldo and Varane took some of the spotlight off the 21-year-old, "both with Raphael Varane and Cristiano coming in, that takes a little bit of pressure off a young man, he's 21, he's learning the game, he's learning how we train, he's learning how we play, he's learning the Premier League, but he's come in hungry to learn. We knew his talent, and we signed him with the thought that we are going to have a top forward here for the next 10 or 12 years. Jadon's finding his feet, it's unfortunate that he fell ill just when he was going to come in, so he was out, and he lost a bit of pre-season. But he is working hard and he will be good."

Once again, Ronaldo was the most transferred in player in FPL for GW5 with over 1.3million managers bringing him into their team.

13: RONALDO SCORES YET AGAIN

Cristiano Ronaldo took his tally to five goals in four Premier League appearances against West Ham but while he's got a good record against the Hammers, it hasn't always gone his way. It was a painful defeat at Upton Park in 2007, where his missed penalty cost Sir Alex Ferguson's side the chance to stay top of the table. Like now, United began the game at the top of the table and Ronaldo was in fine form, and the day started well for United. Ronaldo got on the end of a cross from Ryan Giggs to head United in front, with the Portugal international celebrating in typical flamboyant style.

However, it all went pear shaped in the 66th minute when Ronaldo squandered a glorious chance to double his side's lead. Jonathan Spector handled inside the area, with the referee pointing to the spot. Ronaldo powered his strike wide and was made to regret the miss as West Ham rocked United with two late goals: Anton Ferdinand, up against his brother Rio, equalised after a corner from Mark Noble before Matthew Upson struck late to consign them to a third defeat of the season at the time. Fergie was forced to watch the match from the stands after receiving a ban from the FA.

Rather than criticise Ronaldo after the match, Sir Alex conceded his side had been beaten by the 'better team'. "We were not nearly up to our normal performance. Scoring the penalty would have killed the game but if you lose goals to set pieces you are not at your best. It's difficult to say why but they are human beings and you can't expect them to be perfect all the time." The then West Ham boss Alan Curbishley was ecstatic as he had been forced to field a depleted team following a glut of injuries, but the Hammers were noted for putting up fighting displays against United.

There was a minute's applause at the London Stadium in tribute to Jimmy Greaves, who spent two seasons with West Ham, scoring 13 goals in 40 appearances near the end of his career. Players wore black armbands in tribute. The main tribute would take place later on the Sunday as two of his former clubs, Spurs and Chelsea, squared up at the new Lane.

Ronaldo was back in east London and United fans hailed for his actions during the team's warm-up as he was spotted geeing up his team-mates. Ronaldo was the centre of virtually all the most vital and controversial incidents, expect for one of the major talking points right at the end, in what would have been known as Fergie Time, as United won a thrilling encounter packed full of incident to stay top of the table.

Having fallen behind to deflected shot, Ronaldo scored the equaliser following up a brilliant volleyed flick to tap home the rebound and then had three penalty appeals, two of which looked good enough to give that referee Martin Atkinson waved away. However it was substitute Jesse Lingard who proved the difference with a brilliant 89th minute strike against the club who helped resurrect his career on loan last season. Lingard had received a standing ovation from the home fans after coming on but silenced the crowd when he cut back on to his right foot and hammered the ball past Fabianski, however that proved to be only the start of the drama.

West Ham threw bodies forward in the final moments and a cross was adjudged to have been handled by Luke Shaw and, following a long VAR check, Martin Atkinson awarded the home side a spot-kick. Almost instantly David Moyes brought on Mark Noble to take the penalty. The Hammers legend hadn't missed a spot-kick since 2016 while David De Gea had failed to save his last 40 penalties, including that agonising shoot-out against Villareal in May when he was the one who eventually missed from the spot to hand the Spanish team the trophy. Noble placed his kick to De Gea's left and the Spaniard, helped by Cristiano Ronaldo's gesticulations, guessed correctly and palmed the effort away.

There's little doubts that United deserved all 3 points having dominated the opening period when Bruno Fernandes strike hit a post by Fabianski and forced the Hammers keeper into a string of saves and they were desperately unlucky to fall behind to a wicked deflection that left De Gea stranded. United fought back from that set back quickly and Ronaldo equalised and they continue to dominate before that madcap final few minutes that saw Lingard score and Noble miss the penalty.

Solskjaer's assessment of Ronaldo was simple, "Cristiano arrives at the box as he always does." Ronaldo attempted seven shots at goal from just 41 touches. Five shots were on target. the message was pretty clear, keep providing Ronaldo with the chances and he will deliver. Ronaldo did track back too, at one stage making an overhead kick clearance on the edge of his own box. But Ronaldo's currency is goals and in three games he has now hit four. His United total now stands at 122, overtaking Andy Cole who was on 121.

As far as Solskjaer the first two appeals were "stonewall pens", and left him wondering when Ronaldo is going to get what he deserves in terms of penalties. He was naturally delighted for Lingard who "had a tough evening on Tuesday", but "he knuckled down, he's a positive lad, so happy for him". He delighted in Lingard's turn and finish, and his message to him is that he has to cope with the highs and lows of this game. As for his goalkeeper he was full of prise for that late penalty save, as he confessed that his team looked "down and out" when the spot kick was given, and felt it would have been a genius move for Moyes had that Noble substitution come off, but as it didn't he knew that he would be savaged by some sections of the media/pundits.

Referee Martin Atkinson came in for some huge criticism later that night on Match Of The Day, with pundits Alan Shearer and Dion Dublin re-running the penalty appeals and coming down on the side of Ronaldo. Maybe his past reputation for diving was influencing officials, but with VAR one would have thought it would be much more technical in the approach to deciding whether it is a dive or a penalty.

Solskjaer told the club website: "I'm going to be careful with what I'm saying, but you've got to be wondering what's he's got to do to get a penalty. It's frustrating but they've got to look at it. It's two clear penalties. I think they're stonewall. You can't even argue against them. The first one, he puts his foot out and Ronaldo runs straight and is fouled. The last one, Paul had a foul against him on Zouma when he didn't touch him but he went over him. Why is Cristiano's not? Hopefully it won't be that he's never going to get a penalty."

Victory maintained Ole Gunnar Solskjaer's unbeaten start in the league with four wins and a draw, while West Ham suffered their first loss of the campaign. It could have been so vastly different, it could have ended on a low with dropped points, instead United were still flying high as title contenders. The manager, though, declined to get drawn into talk about title chances and sarcastically said that he was 'losing my job yesterday' after their shock Champions League defeat in midweek.

Solskjaer has been under constant scrutiny since taking the United job on a full-time basis back in 2019, but now he faced persistent comments from pundits that he should be axed if he fails to deliver silverware this season; his position was again questioned in midweek when United suffered a disappointing 2-1 loss at Swiss side Young Boys. United legends including Rio Ferdinand, Peter Schmeichel and Paul Scholes speculated that the manager's job was in peril unless he delivered silverware. Solskjaer kept his cool, even if his sense of humour was wearing thin, when he was asked about United's title credentials when he reminded the interviewer that his future was being questioned only a few days ago. "You're not going to get me on that one now," he replied, "it's five games into the season. I was probably down and out and lost my job yesterday. That's the way it is at United. We deserved three points. It's a hard place to come, here. Hopefully these points can make a difference. Let's see [about the title] when we get towards April and May.'

The manager was thrilled with the attacking football, especially the way his side responded to going a goal down, and he was happy with the movement, but he wanted his team to work better defensively, and clearly that was an area he earmarked for vast improvement that would take place on the training ground. He added: "We have to defend better. We have to make it harder to break us down. For their goal the structure was wrong for whatever reason and we'll have to work on it."

Whatever the shortcomings, given the circumstances surrounding the finish, it was hard not to believe that it was all about the Ronaldo Effect. Mark Noble is one of the most prolific penalty takers in Premier League history, he has scored 27 goals from the spot, the fourth highest in the competition's history, converting 84.4% of the 32 he has attempted. David de Gea's record of saving spot kicks was excreable, he'd not stopped one since October 2014 in the league, a run of 21 penalties. In fact it was his first penalty save in any competition since 2016. As Jimmy Greaves himself would often say: "it's a funny old game".

While Solskjaer raced over to join the celebrations and congratulations for the keeper, Ronaldo was one of the first to do that, and his influence within the squad was becoming clear. There seemed to be a belief that this would be a remarkable, special season. Ronaldo, himself, well he was relishing it all, having talked about his love for English football, all the drama, the kind he had played his part in at West Ham, the competitiveness he didn't find very often in Italy or Spain, when he posted on Instagram to his 345million followers....

"Every game in the Premier League is always an amazing fight for the three points. Today we got to see a glimpse of all the obstacles that we will find on our way, but we have to keep our mind set on our goals. 'Together! Strong! Focused! Let's go, Devils!"

The post, viewed 10 million times, was followed by a muscle emoji and those muscle were carrying Ronaldo toward the age of 40 without any sign of slowing down his reflexes in front of goal.

14: CHEAT OR VICTIM?

"Let's be fair, he had three penalty claims in the match with West Ham and deserved to have had two at least"

KEITH HACKETT

I s Cristiano Ronaldo a cheat or a victim? Quite clearly he is seen as a legitimate target for defenders, to wind up or simply kick if they can get away with it. Sometimes Ronaldo goes down in the box with minimal contact, and is often accused of diving but is it diving or a legitimate tool for a forward to strike back at defenders who are guilty of 'dangling a leg' or making a rash last ditch tackle inside the box?

When Ronaldo first burst onto the scene at Old Trafford there were a profusion of controversial incidents and numerous accusation of diving. In the League Cup final against Spurs Ronaldo was fouled by Ledley King in the box and Referee Chris Foy raised a yellow card straight away for what is sometimes called 'simulation', often called cheating. Ronaldo tumbled over a lunge from King in the area and although his fall was theatrical there was no doubt contact was made. It could easily have been a penalty, instead Ronaldo was shown the yellow card. Ronaldo should have been celebrating a penalty when Ledley King stretched and stamped on his right foot as he raced along the edge of the box. Ronaldo doesn't make it easy for himself with his antics, but that was a clear penalty. Ronaldo got there a fraction before King who stood on his toe and sent him over. Ledley King applauded the referee for booking Ronaldo for diving but it was the wrong decision. There was no VAR in those days to over turn the decision yet even with VAR three penalty appeals against West Ham were waved away when a VAR review would have seen justice done.

The big question is whether Ronaldo suffers due to his reputation for diving, and whether that reputation is justified. Ole Gunnar Solskjaer made a big effort to avoid controversy in his post-match comments and put it in as gentle a way was he could by saying he hoped that this was just an isolate episode and not a sign of things to come.

Yet Jamie O'Hara accused Ronaldo of diving against the Hammers as replays showed he was on his way down before the contact came from former Chelsea defender Kurt Zouma while Rangers legend Ally McCoist claimed that Ronaldo was right to go down and that Zouma had made a clumsy decision to dive in.

As the Talksport debate raged, McCoist came down on the side of a fellow striker, strikers are told that if they feel contact they should go down, few stay on their feet, "It is a penalty. Zouma dived in. Your natural instinct as a player is to protect yourself. Zouma is late. It's a rash challenge. It's a penalty" while O'Hara accused Ronaldo of diving, "The contact is there because he's anticipated Zouma coming in. Just take the tackle. Zouma dives in. Take the tackle and then it's a penalty. The fact that you go down before you feel the contact, you're diving. That's not a penalty. He's running at pace. Yes, he's pushed it past Zouma but if you look closely and watch from all angles, he's already on his way down. He's dived. He's looking for the penalty."

Ole Gunnar Solskjaer agreed with McCoist and thought United should've been awarded a penalty for the challenge by Zouma on Ronaldo. "The first one and the third one, I think they are stonewall and you can't even argue against them. The first one, the lad puts his foot out and Cristiano runs straight. And why is Cristiano's third appeal not a penalty? I hope it won't be 'Cristiano is never going to get a penalty'."

Ronaldo's early days were littered with accusations of diving and that reputation followed him to Spain where he was yellow carded for simulation against Rayo Vallecano – despite clear contact – before he went on to score his 300th goal for the club. Perhaps that reputation weighed on the mind of the referee when Antonio Amaya slid into Ronaldo's legs inside the hosts' penalty area in the 51st minute. The visiting fans were expecting a penalty in what looked to be one of the easier spot-kick decisions of the season – but the official instead yellow-carded the Ballon d'Or holder for what he considered a dive. Ronaldo was stunned to be booked.

To get right to the heart of the matter, I contacted a couple of the games most experienced and respected referees. Dermott Gallagher made it clear that at no time would he have considered the reputation of Ronaldo or indeed any player, he officiated, to cloud his judgement, "I am referring an England v Wales over 70s game and will treat them all the same on the day, with equal respect. That is how I have always refereed. That would apply to Ronaldo or any player. I would have referred Ronaldo for around four years from the time that he started out at Manchester United as a teenager, and I cannot tell you anything about him as I would have treated him the same as any player I would have referred. All I can recall is that I didn't award a penalty for him, or indeed book him for diving.

"The issue with referring is that every decision is subjective, even the decisions from VAR, it all comes down to opinion as opposed to factual decisions, and that applies to every player being treated them same. What happened with Ronaldo in the West Ham game is no different to what happened to Walker at Manchester City and whether he should have been sent off, it all comes down to a subjective view of the referee. All I know is that in all my years as a referee I was never biased toward Ronaldo, never been biased toward any player. As a referee you apply the laws of the game equally to any player, and I would never have had it any other way and never have it now any other way even if it applies to an over 70s games between England and Wales. Would I have been influenced by a players reputation? The answer is a definite no I wouldn't, and never have been in the 14 years I was a referee."

Keith Hackett is one of the greatest referees of all time, once one of FIFA's top and most prominent officials. He took charge at some of the most important matches including the FA Cup Final at Wembley, European Championships as well as countless top flight games and even refereed at the Olympics. "In my view when you are a top referee, taking charge of a top game, you get yourself prepared, you want to understand that players you will be controlling, aware of their tactics. When it comes to the world's best players you want to make sure you give them proper protection because you know there are some defenders who will pursue certain tactics to try to put them out of the game. So the ref has got to come prepared, to know what might confront them. That is not to say pre-judge, or to be influenced by spectators.

"A player like Ronaldo is not easy to referee, top

players can often make life difficult for the ref. Often they can be accused of simulation, going down looking for a penalty, put quite bluntly they could be out to deceive the ref, you have to be aware of that. Often a ref would err on the defender's side and issue a yellow card for simulation, effectively accusing the player of cheating."

Keith, though, had no worries about controlling the world's best players, he found it a challenge, one he would rise to and overcome. "We are lucky to have world class players in the Premier League, like Ronaldo, it enhances our game, not just for the club, but for the entire league. We have enjoyed exceptionally talented players. The greatest players of our time has been Ronaldo and Lionel Messi and we have been lucky to have had Ronaldo in our country, one of the greatest players of his era, a player you would mention in the same breath as players in previous eras such as Pele, Maradona, Platini. These type of players are exciting and entertaining, but for referees they are challenging, they are a freak of nature, they can be a handful. Players such as Gazza, he was a player of immense talent and enthusiasm, but enthusiasm that can sometimes go over the top."

For Keith Hackett the Ronaldo of his first spell in English football is vastly different to the new mature version, and for that reason he has seen a big improvement in the way he reacts on the field. "Early in his career he would go to ground too easily for my liking in a bid to win free kicks and penalties to benefit his team and to benefit himself. Now, though, he has matured. He is a presence on the field, and he has earned the right to be a presence through his extraordinary abilities. He has made incredible sacrifices to have reached that level.

"Early in his career I was visiting Alex Ferguson at Carrington and saw Ronaldo on the training ground, out there long after everyone else has left, practising those free kicks, you could see that remarkable natural talent but a talent that he spent hours and hours perfecting on the training pitch. He had that ability but worked hard to hone it to give him that extra edge. You could see why he would want free kicks in and around the penalty area, he was so dangerous from those positions.

"At times, in those early days, he could be confrontational during a game with the ref. at those times it is imperative the ref remains calm and manages the players. Ronaldo demanded fairness, he thought he had been unfairly treated if he didn't get those free kicks. In those circumstances I always felt it best to talk to the captains to calm things down and try to influence a better approach from him. It takes two to argue, so don't argue with him is the best way for the ref to maintain control.

"In those early days you should look at his stats because he was defending the ball on his goal line one minute and then popping up and scoring at the other end. A real team player. Yet he was selfish at the same time because he wanted to get to the very top, he wanted to be top goalscorer, and he was very focused on fulfilling his aims. For a referee you needed to be totally focused and concentrated to make the right calls.

"When Ronaldo gets on the ball you know something might happen but it is important not to pre-judge anything. You know from your preparation that he wants to score, he will want to stay on his first, he will want to go by the defender, but you also know if he can't, he might go for the third option and go to ground. It's challenging for the ref, but equally, although it might be tough, it is worth it, because you are dealing with a rare talent, an extra special world class player.

"I can he has now matured on his return to Manchester United. He no longer is someone who has to prove himself, and he is far more conservative in his approach, in the incidents when he had claimed a penalty he hasn't found the need any more to chase after the referee and shout and scream at him. All we have seen is Ronaldo sitting there with a wry smile on his face.

"Let's be fair, he made three penalty claims in the match with West Ham and deserved to have had two at least. One of them you would expect the ref in the local park to have given it, it was that clear cut! You have to worry that it is possible that Ronaldo is being pre judged, that his reputation has gone before him, and is behind judged accordingly. You have to ask the question whether the referees are being influenced by his reputation.

"This is the reason I brought in one of the very best sports psychologists when I was at the Professional Game Match Official Limited Limited (PGMOL) group that officiate all Premier League matches after Mark Clattenburg retired early because he was under so much pressure. Fans think that Manchester United are given everything, far too many penalties, and you cannot escape it, and referees will sub consciously go into those high profile games thinking about that, thinking about Ronaldo's reputation. They don't want to pre-judge anything, they want to be fair, but it must be somewhere in the mind of the referee it is is unavoidable. Refs want to be fair, and they set out to be fair, but certainly with someone like Ronaldo the debate will rage on whether they are being fair to him or not. I believe that referees set out to be fair but the very best in the world can do unexpected things, and Ronaldo is one of the modern player in the game, he can go down easy, but I feel this is now less so.

"VAR is there now also to help making the right decision, but I'm afraid even VAR is suffering in sync with the ref on the spot. VAR sees Ronaldo in exactly the same way as the ref would do. It is hard not to pre-judge. VAR is no different to the ref in that respect. Both for the ref and indeed for VAR, the level of awareness has to rise."

15: WHO IS THE G.O.A.T.?

"I do think he's the greatest football player that has ever lived. That is not a bias."

GARY NEVILLE

The Greatest Player of All Time? Well, for me it has to be Pele. Of course I have met Pele many times, and with his approval wrote the first biography of the great man some time ago. However, there is no doubt that Ronaldo and Messi have generated numerous debates whether they have overtaken, not only Pele, but also Diego Maradona. Peter Crouch was forced to reconsider his opinions, having "always been a Lionel Messi man", whom he described as "a gift from God" with attributes "poise, elegance and everything that goes with his genius is spellbinding", but he has suddenly switched to Ronaldo. The reason? The way Ronaldo was breaking virtually every record in the book.

Gary Neville bias shone through when he selected Ronaldo as his G.O.A.T, while his Sky rival Jamie Carragher insisted Lionel Messi is the greatest footballer of all time. Neville played with Ronaldo for six years at United between 2003 and 2009. Red Nev said: "I've always ignored the Ronaldo and Messi question, it's a bit of a fantasy and both need to be enjoyed. I was asked this morning by a gentleman who was driving me in: If you could pick any player in history to come off the bench and win you a game, who would it be? It would absolutely be Cristiano Ronaldo. I do think he's the greatest football player that has ever lived. That is not a bias. Messi is a ridiculous player who's scored an obscene amount of goals. It's incredibly similar (on the stats) apart from the wrong-footed goals, the headers, and the penalties. That takes me to a point whereby he's more complete in terms of the most important part of the game. What tips me is the international record, the most goals of all-time, and the five Champions Leagues with worse teams than Messi's."

Jamie Carragher disagreed however, "Ronaldo is not the greatest player of all time. I'm going to say it's his mate here (Messi). It doesn't matter how a ball goes in the net, Messi has more goals than Ronaldo. Messi is also a playmaker, he can run a game, Ronaldo can't do that. Talk about who you want coming off the bench, Messi has scored more goals coming off the bench, so that's a ridiculous thing you've said there. Ronaldo does things other players can do, Messi does things we've never seen before. In terms of the goalscoring that's not right. There's been a lot of fanfare about Ronaldo from ex-players, I just think you've just got carried away."

Rio Ferdinand called the achievement or reaching 100 goals for his country as 'crazy'. Rio said: "Some players don't even get 100 goals in their whole career. This isn't even about your club goals, this is just the national team. It's crazy." However in the authorised biography of Pele, the Brazil legend told me during many interviews with him, "when they made Pele, they broke the mould". There would never be another Pele." Ronaldo and Messi certainly have come close.

Perhaps the last word should go to Sir Alex Ferguson. Back in 2015 he was asked about the merits of Ronaldo v Messi. Since both have moved clubs the early signs would appear to favour Cristiano as Messi did not register a goal or an assist for Paris Saint-Germain in his first few games after leaving Barcelona after 21 years at the club while Ronaldo got off to a flying start back at United. The former United boss always thought Messi could only achieve the numbers he has playing for Barcelona. "People say who is the best player in the world? And plenty of people quite rightly say Messi – you can't dispute that opinion but Ronaldo could play for Millwall, Queens Park Rangers, Doncaster Rovers... anyone, and score a hat-trick in a game. I'm not sure Messi could do it. I think Messi is a Barcelona player, you know what I mean?"

Ronaldo jumped to No. 1 in the Forbes highest paid footballers in the world list finally overtaking his biggest commercial rival Lionel Messi. His potential earnings for the first season of his return to Manchester United were put at an eye watering £91.5million. Messi's move to France could see him earn £80.5m this season. For the first time, Ronaldo and Messi, two of the most high-profile players in the history of football, made transfer moves at the same time; Ronaldo to United, Messi to Paris St Germain.

Ronaldo was in line to earn £51.25m in basic salary at old Trafford, plus lucrative performance-related bonuses. But there are also vast commercial income from multiple endorsements, including sponsorship. Messi has a higher basic salary and bonus structure than Ronaldo of £54.94m per year at PSG, but only collects £25.6m in annual sponsorship payments, compared to Ronaldo's yearly sum of £40m. Only!

Messi had intended to stay at Barcelona and had agreed new terms, but incredibly Barca let him leave on a free transfer because they could not afford to keep him. He might have remained Forbes' highest-paid footballer as his total earnings in Spain was £95.24m per year, but he had agreed to halve his wages because he wanted to stay, but even that wasn't enough due to the major financial issues at the club, who let him go and then announced a debt of £1.15billion. Both Messi and Ronaldo will earn less this season than during previous years, despite new contracts following their moves. Ronaldo was just behind Messi on last season's list released in May, earning a £87.91m overall potential package including endorsements.

16: NO RONALDO - NO HOPE

It didn't take long for United fans to realise: no Ronaldo, no hope. The presence of Ronaldo on the team sheet can spread fear among the opposition, but the sight of Ronaldo missing from the team-sheet clearly has the opposite effect as West Ham's two results against Manchester United proved – with Ronaldo in the opposition they were fortunate to get away with a 2-1 defeat, when he was rested for the League Cup tie 3 days later they deservedly won 1-0 at Old Trafford.

The League Cup might have been bottom of the list of priorities but without a trophy as manager, the opportunity to at least land the League Cup disappeared with an unexpected defeat. Solskjaer explained why it was essential to rest Ronaldo and several other first team regulars for the cup tie in the quick repeat fixture with West Ham, as he made 11 changes to the side that beat them in the league. Nothing unusual there. In fact there were 160 changes in total from the 18 Premier League teams in the Carabao Cup third round ties with West Ham manager David Moyes making quite a few himself. Ronaldo, Pogba, Maguire, Varane and de Gea were among the top players left out of the entire squad with only a couple of A listers on the bench.

When Ronaldo walked through the Old Trafford car park ahead of the game he was welcomed by a plethora of fans, who cheered his arrival. He seemed keen to go over to the supporters, even gesturing with his hand that he wanted to sign autographs but an official dressed in a suit and walking behind him moved him on, preventing him from spending any time with the fans. Ronaldo looked disappointed and gave the fans a wave and a thumbs up as he continued walking past them to the stadium.

The manager had decided virtually immediately after the league game on Sunday to make wholesale changes for the Wednesday night cup tie, explaining that "we need more players to get match fit". Discussing Ronaldo's absence he said: "Cristiano has come in and made a difference already, he wants to play as much as possible but I don't think it is possible. If you are going to be successful at the end, you need the whole squad and minutes to be shared out. It's a risk making so many changes but we have played some games behind closed doors and hopefully we find the rhythm."

West Ham gained instant revenge for their home defeat with Manuel Lanzini's ninth-minute winner, his first goal in almost 12 months and only his second since May 2019. A delighted Moyes' took his team into the last 16. The second-half introductions of Bruno Fernandes and Mason Greenwood failed to land an equaliser and the questions were inevitably raised whether Solskjaer possessed sufficient strength in depth.

The Hammers first Old Trafford triumph since Carlos Tevez's matchwinner in 2007 that kept them in the Premier League, and the first in a cup competition since Paolo di Canio scored the only goal in an FA Cup meeting in 2001, highlighted that the manager could only rely on his first choice team with Ronaldo as the inspirational figure.

Solskjaer picked a completely different side, yet they were all internationals. Some of his fringe players made it plain to the manager that it was time to move on, and they could make no complaints if, at best, they ended up with a place on the bench. Anthony Martial was a peripheral figure in attack, Juan Mata was replaced by Fernandes in the second-half, while Lingard, who like Mata has a contract that expires in the summer, was not at his best while Dean Henderson did little to help his pre season belief that he would mount a realistic threat to David de Gea as first choice keeper.

There was even controversy surrounding a penalty decision - yet, Ronaldo was no where to be seen! Solskjaer wanted a first-half penalty after Mark Noble's challenge on Lingard. It was a clear penalty, argued Solskjaer as he insisted Noble falls and pulls him down, "We don't seem to be getting decisions at the moment" complained the United boss.

For Solskjaer it was a tough defeat as it brought to a swift end any early hopes of securing the first available silverware of the season, and ending the wait for a trophy stretching back to 2017. The only positive he tired to take from it was that it was important to get some of his fringe players "up to speed"

Fans lost patience with Martial with one Twitter user commenting, "If 36-year-old Cristiano Ronaldo could track back, defend and run up and down the pitch, what excuse does 25-year-old Anthony Martial have? Slow, uninterested and static up front. Makes it hard to defend him." Others wondered where Edinson Cavani had disappeared to.

17: THE RONALDO EFFECT

"We have some new coaches at the club who were wondering if we might get 40,000 people turning up in the Carabao Cup. We explained to them that it would virtually be full and sure enough the place was packed and the atmosphere was exceptional."

OLE GUNNAR SOLSKJAER

It seemed that the Ronaldo Effect was even being felt in the Manchester City dressing room. His mere presence, added to his profusion of goals right at the start of his second coming at Old Trafford, had produced an incredible reaction even in their biggest rivals camp. He had made Manchester United a vastly different proposition in the title race, according to his Portugal team-mate Ruben Dias, one of Manchester City's most influential players, a key performer when Pep Guardiola's side won back the title last season.

Ronaldo had been widely tipped to join City and the fact that one of the most powerful club sides in the world missed out on signing Harry Kane when they offered £120 million and Spurs held out for £150 million which City refused to pay, and then missed out on signing Ronaldo, City endured a mixed start to the new season. Having said that City didn't have a good start but recovered to win the title, so couldn't be discounted. Having lost Sergio Aguero to Barcelona and without a recognised No.9, an opening day defeat at Tottenham and a goalless draw at home to Southampton left United, Liverpool and Chelsea jointly top of the table.

"Cristiano, year after year, continues to be at a high level," said Dias, "he has come up big again. He returns to one of the most competitive leagues in the world and to one of the clubs with the most ambitions. It's a big step for him. We won't be predicting the future, but obviously United come out reinforced and become more and more a strong candidate."

Former United captain Roy Keane might be delighted with the arrival of Ronaldo, certainly after his blistering start, but he wanted more players to step up and he warned that the team cannot just rely on Ronaldo to constantly deliver. That was evident, Keane argued, when he was looking forward to a good result in the Champions League at Young Boys, but Ronaldo was made to struggled upfront without getting "decent support or possession". "Man United have to be careful because Ronaldo's come to the club everyone thinks it's just going to fall into place, the players still need to step up and do better than what they had in the one or two years but he's still a world class player."

Cristiano Ronaldo was an inspiration for a variety of sportsmen including Anthony Joshua, but he also inspired opponents to want to deliver a knock out punch when they faced him; it was a double edge sword for Untied, he was a match winner in his own right but he also galvanised the opposition to raise their game had an inspiring effect on opponents. The age old Liverpool-United rivalry was re-ignited in far more real terms as both were going head to head in the title race, alongside Chelsea and City.

Diogo Jota expressed the view that Ronaldo's return to the Premier League would only add more spice to fixtures between the two biggest clubs in England this season. Jota grew up idolising Ronaldo and now plays alongside him for the Portugal national team and he admitted that United were now equipped with a 'strong weapon' as a result of Ronaldo's arrival and he was excited by the prospect of the two clubs contesting the title. "Unfortunately, he is playing against us," the Liverpool forward admitted. The Portuguese striker has been one of Jurgen Klopp's surprise signings and cemented his place in the team with some crucial goals but was aware that Ronaldo "can score from nothing, he just scores" which makes him "a very strong weapon that the enemy now have. It will just be another thing to spice the game up. In the end, that's what all the fans want and hopefully we come out with the win in those games."

Aston Villa right back Matty Cash headed off to Old Trafford brimming full of confidence having scored in their last game, their second win of the season a 3-0 victory over Everton, eager to defend against Ronaldo when he said: "Everyone knows how good Ronaldo is, so playing against him will be unreal and trying to stop him at the same time. Sharing the same pitch as Ronaldo is an honour. He's had a great start but I'm part of a defence which has to stop him. For me, playing against Ronaldo today, the greatest footballer ever, is just part of a crazy journey my career has taken me on such Wycombe released me."

Cristiano packs a knock out punch in front of goal, and has met Anthony Joshua in Dubai and the UK. Joshua talked to Rio Ferdinand about the success of Ronaldo, and their mutual respect. "That's what I find interesting, him joining Man United is a tough ask, it's a lot of pressure that he's gonna be under, but it's different in boxing, you can't have a little last dance. It's like me having two pints and laying flat on the floor after getting knocked out. There ain't no last dance. That's the mental thing with boxing. If you have got your last dance in your mind, you've gotta give everything you've got. What I think when you're saying all this stuff with Ronaldo, like the chef, in my head it seems like a perfect world, he must have had it nice. Being great is having to go that extra mile time and time again. But it's because when you face that adversity, you've lived in this comfort putting yourself at every advantage that you can. So when you're in adversity you can pull yourself out at the last minute. For me, hearing all that stuff, I'm not looking at it like, 'He lived a happy life, chef, masseuse.' He just knew how tough it was and he wanted to pull himself out of those tough times, so he went the extra mile."

Ronaldo spoken on a documentary with Joshua's broadcaster DAZN about a conversation they had on holiday in Dubai. "We had the opportunity to speak last year in Dubai, I was with Joshua and we had a conversation," Ronaldo told Gennady Golovkin on Parallel Worlds. "Thirty-three years old is that age where you start to feel down. I don't wanna be in the sport, in football, where people say, 'Cristiano was an unbelievable player and now he's slow'. I don't want that. You can take care a lot of your body, the body's not a problem I don't think. Between watching a football match or a boxing or UFC fight, I choose boxing or UFC. I don't think I could have been a boxer, it's tough. You have to be born for that, with that gift."

Joshua explained the impact of Ronaldo's resilience on his own ambitions, despite conceding defeat in chasing a similar "dream". "He's only kicking a football, isn't he? What a man," Joshua told the Metro. "We always compare ourselves to the one in a billion: he's one in a billion and we always seem to compare ourselves to that guy. I can't chase the Cristiano Ronaldo dream. Cristiano is one of the people I see asking for strength and courage. It comes with hardship but at the end of it is self-satisfaction. I think you've got between 36 and 40. So at 36 it's kind of like, how many more years do you go beyond that? Do you do the full yard to 40? Forty seems like the age where it's like, 'okay, you've done this for a long time now'. So yeah, 36 to 40 is when I look at my career.'

For Raphael Varane it was a pleasure to play alongside Ronaldo having rekindled a friendship they had for seven years at Real Madrid. The striker has an aura surrounding him after achieving so much and a massive "example" that way applies himself with an incredible work ethic. "Cristiano Ronaldo? He's a huge pro. He has been marked his entire career and he will be so as long as he plays football. It's better to have him with us than against. If he is still at the highest level at his age, it is not for nothing. It's great to be able to work, play, have fun with him. And we know him, he's made to win, to score goals, so it's better to have him with you. We know the aura he has."

Solskjaer must treat Ronaldo differently according to former defender Jaap Stam, the former treble winner. Stam said "If you bring in a player like this at the age that he is, you cannot say to Cristiano, 'Hey, I'm the manager, you listen to me and do what I want.' He is a grown-up, an adult, he's 36 years old so you need to treat him with a lot of respect for what he's done and what he can do for you to help you out. Ole is going to be in talks with Cristiano daily in how to get the best out of him, and what he can do [for the team to] provide more balls for Cristiano to score.

The important thing for United is that Ole uses Ronaldo in a way where he can hopefully do less, but still hopefully score a lot of goals."

Ronaldo's presence would benefit youngsters as an example of how to keep yourself fit and how to reach the top. Stam didn't consider Ronaldo selfish and instead he was someone who would actively want to encourage the younger players to help them and talk to his team-mates about what to do, and also not being selfish for himself but giving others the opportunities to score when he can't. Stam said: "That tells you something about a player of his stature and his professionalism. When he comes in, the whole club changes a little bit and there's probably a different feeling."

A goalkeeper who couldn't save a penalty to save his life, had suddenly saved a penalty to keep United top of the pile, could be put down to good fortune, the kind of luck Sir Alex was always accused of possessing in far too excessive qualities. Maybe it was all part of the Ronaldo Effect, a belief that anything was possible when this guy returned. Certainly, without any doubt, Ronaldo's impact stretched beyond his excellent goalscoring form, but whether it actually had some mystical effect on David De Gea seems a touch fanciful.

However, De Gea has had his say ahead of the latest round of Premier League games, when he commented: "It's amazing to have him back at home. He's already a legend in the club, so I think for the players, for the young lads, for everyone, he's a great guy to see every day how he works in the gym, how he treats himself, how he takes care of his body, and of himself. He is an amazing player and it's great to see him here every day working hard and helping the team.'

De Gea has no doubt that the arrival of Ronaldo and other key signings will end a trophy drought that stretches back to the 2017 Europa League final. "Let's see, like I said, now we have a bigger squad, big players – players with experience like Cristiano, like Raphael Varane, like me, Juan Mata – so we have more experience on the team. So let's see, it can be a great year. We signed good players and we already had a good squad. We are there at the top of the league fighting for every game, of course it is hard, it is the best league in the world. Every game is difficult, we want to fight for the big trophies, try to fight for the Premier League, the Champions League, for everything. I think we have the squad and the players and we have the fans with us so it's amazing. I think the club is in a good point."

Ronaldo was the driving force behind Manchester United's title drive, and to prove it he drove a new £164,000 luxury Bentley to the club's training ground the morning after his side crashed out of the Carabao Cup with his two personal bodyguards following very closely behind in another car. Ronaldo didn't play and could be seen in the crowd growing visibly frustrated as his team squandered chances. He watched United's 27 shots, only six of which were on target.

Edinson Cavani was finally ready for consideration with the intriguing OAP partnership up front with Ronaldo. The Uruguayan joined in training fully after the cup defeat and Solskjaer confessed he was excited to see them together, as he felt both were goal scorers of the highest calibre and together would be a handful for defences, especially against sides who dropped deep to deny United space.

Ronaldo inherited the number seven shirt from

Cavani, who had played just once in the last 12 weeks since Uruguay were eliminated from the Copa America and he has been sidelined for the last two weeks after sustaining an injury during the international fortnight.

With Chelsea v Manchester City the big match of the weekend, there was a great chance for Liverpool and United to establish themselves as front runners. Solskjaer, though, stressed that while it was early in the season the first two months were vital to establish their credentials as realistic challengers. Getting a head start always builds momentum as he observed

"It's been a decent return with 13 points", but he felt there were areas of his team to work on and "bigger challenges ahead" he admitted however that United needed to stop conceding the first goal. "I've sent a letter to the Premier League asking if we can start games 1-0 down. It will make it so much easier for us. Joking apart, it's a big, big part of the game and we need to start better. We can't expect to come back and win games as we have done fantastically in the last 12, 14, 15 months, but that's going to catch up with us."

Solskjaer used his programme notes to demand a fast start from his players. United led for a total of just 50 minutes in four top-flight games. "I'd like us to address the slow starts because we've been making to games because we don't want that setting in and becoming an issue," writes Solskjaer. He paid tribute to fans who have made an "unbelievable atmosphere" at Old Trafford. "We have some new coaches at the club who were wondering if we might get 40,000 people turning up in the Carabao Cup. We explained to them that it would virtually be full and sure enough the place was packed and the atmosphere was exceptional."

Without a single penalty this season and Ronaldo especially picked out as suffering for failure to gain one when it looked stitched on, Solskjaer blamed Jurgen Klopp. He pointed out there was a marked difference in penalties for United since the Klopp complained in January that United had 'had more penalties in two years than I had in five-and-a-half-years'. Klopp made the remark when he was furious when Sadio Mane was denied a penalty in Liverpool's 1-0 defeat at Southampton and United had just pulled level on points with Liverpool though Fernandes's winning penalty against Aston Villa.

United were awarded 11 penalties in the Premier League last season, five after Klopp's outburst at the start of the year. Solskjaer just hoped that his team would get what they deserved, implying that they had not got what the deserved in terms of adequate penalties. Solskjaer reiterated that his teams should have had three penalties in the last two games. "There was a certain manager last year who was starting to worry about us getting pens and after that it seems like the decisions are more difficult to give. I've seen a big, big difference since then. We just have to leave it to the refs and hopefully they'll make the right calls very soon."

The manager was "delighted" with the instant impact but he pointed out that "he's a different man now to when I played with him. He's been absolutely top. Work-rate, his attitude into games, communication. He knows he's not going to play every game but that's a good chat to have with me when he feels like he won't be ready."

Ronaldo turns 37 in February, and Solskjaer doesn't see him slowing down, "not at all, because of the way he looks after himself. That's the key to it - and of course some genes. There must be some genes as well, some DNA in there. He has put every single ounce of energy and effort into becoming the player he is and has been, so he deserves every single little plaudit that he gets for his physical state. What's more impressive is when you have achieved as much as he has, he's still as hungry. His mentality is still absolutely spot-on and that's a desire from inside that he's going to keep going until his head says, 'no, I've given everything now'. Hopefully it will last a few more years."

Solskjaer pointed to Linford Christie who won the Olympic 100m aged 32 in 1992 as being "quite an age" for a sprinter to win gold, 'so age is never a problem.' Solskjaer's former team-mate Ryan Giggs played beyond his 40th birthday, and the feeling was that Ronaldo can emulate that feat. "He's still one of the quickest players in the league", added Ole, "but of course he's back into the Premier League and there's maybe more intensity than the Italian and the Spanish leagues, so we'll have to manage his workload. But he's there to score goals, of course, and to create goals.'

Solskjaer was sure that the rest in the week meant key players such as Ronaldo were fresh, prepared well, having worked well throughout the week, despite a few needed on the bench in midweek. "Early kick-offs... It's hard when you play Wednesday night. That's part of the reason we did what we did on Wednesday night." the manager reverted to the team that beat West Ham in the league with one of the notable changes on the substitute's bench; Edinson Cavani. The United boss added: "He is an exceptional striker, finisher, his movement in the box. Tight games are always decided in the boxes so to have another striker is good."

Mark Lawrenson still had many question marks against United's credentials to land the title, but as he did his usual pre-match predictions for the BBC on line, he felt "Bruno Fernandes is going to be on form for United, and Cristiano Ronaldo is going to enjoy himself too." He went for a 2-1 United win as he commented: "Manchester United are still not quite right for me. They are going to win a load of games this season, but there will be times where they unexpectedly come unstuck."

Most pundits went for a home win, as Villa had won just one of their past 45 Premier League games against United and arrived at Old Trafford seeking a first away point this season. However, most pundits would have gone for more than a one goal margin. As well as being one of only three Premier League sides unbeaten alongside Liverpool and Chelsea, United scored more than any other side in the league so far.

18: UNITED PAY THE PENALTY

"This is only the beginning, but in a competition as strong as the Premier League, every point counts! We must react immediately, get back on our feet and show our true strength"

CRISTIANO RONALDO

Cristiano Ronaldo had yet another major record in his sights; the first post-war United player to score in their first four appearances after signing for the club. Romelu Lukaku had taken a penalty in his fourth appearance for United against Leicester, but his spot kick was saved by Kasper Schmeichel. The last United player to score in his first four appearances for the club was James Hanson in 1924. Ronaldo, of course, had his first four games back in 2003 but if he scored this time he would become the first post-war United signing to score in their 'first' four matches. The team Ronaldo scored most of his United goals against? Aston Villa! Eight goals against them in his first spell at United.

On a typical grey Manchester morning a huge roar erupted around the ground to welcome the players for their pre-match warm-up before the 12.30 kick off. Lots of Ronaldo songs from the home fans as you would expect. They are all big games, but it was a big game having made an early exit from the Carabao Cup in midweek, they needed a morale boaster before Villarreal's visit in the Champions League, a repeat of last season's Europa League final, while title favourites Chelsea, at least Alan Shearer thought so, kicked off at the same time against City. Two huge games for the top of the table with Liverpool at Brentford in the evening start.

But despite the sun breaking through the clouds the first half was goalless with Villa spurning the better chances to take the lead. Perhaps Solskjaer had seen the light and would make early substitutions with the fans wanting to see Ronaldo paired up front with Cavani

Villa started the second half as they'd finished the first and threatened to break through several times only to be denied by the flag of the linesman and some last-ditch defending. With just 10 minutes of normal time remaining Cavani replaced Scott McTominay but almost immediately Villa started to dominate the ball and forced a succession of corner before Kortney Hause glanced home at the near post past David de Gea – it was poor defending but Villa fully deserved their lead.

Within minutes United laid siege to the Stretford End goal, a cross came in which was blocked by a defender's arm and Mike Dean immediately pointed to the spot. The question on everyone's lips was who would take it. Straightaway Bruno Fernandes claimed the ball and steadied himself to take it but unbelievably skied it miles over the bar. Of course the one thought on everyone's mind after that was - why didn't Ronaldo take it? Well, Bruno's success rate from the spot is 93% and Ronaldo's 83% so perhaps the manager knew best.

It all meant a first Premier League defeat of the season for United as Villa get their first league win at Old Trafford since 2009. The ramifications were tough to take. United dropped to fourth as the same points as Chelsea and City, following the sky blues win at Stamford Bridge although Liverpool, who faced Brentford later that afternoon, did their rivals a favour by twice squandering a lead to draw a frenetic game 3-3 and so led the table by just a point.

Ole Gunnar Solskjaer complained bitterly that Villa's goal shouldn't have stood as it was offside, so it was hard to take. VAR made the decision to allow Villa's goal even though striker Ollie Watkins was standing close to de Gea. "You can see the inconsistency again, VAR and decision-making. Watkins is standing on or touching David as the header has gone in so it's a foul or he is offside. The linesman did his job he called it into VAR but they turned the decision down and it is a goal unfortunately, so bad decisions again." He also compared it to a recent goal of almost identical situation that ruled two Leicester City goals offside although MOTD analysis indicated that the United keeper wasn't impeded and that Watkins wasn't in his line of vision. What was noted was the lack of a full back on the post which would have prevented the goal.

Goalkeeper Emiliano Martinez goaded Ronaldo, pointing at him, egging him on to take the penalty. "You take it, why don't you take it". Captain of the team and Ronaldo's Portuguese team mate Bruno Fernandez seemed unfazed, as Ronaldo refused to be intimidated by the keeper. However, it seemed as though Martinez had got into their heads as Fernandez abandoned his usual hop and a skip run up style that had given him incredible penalty stats of 22 out of 23 successes, Fernandes only missed one of his penalties for United when Newcastle's Karl Darlow denied him in October.

Instead of his highly successful placement, he opted for power and was well wide of the target, Chris Waddle style, lifting the shot well over the bar, blasting the ball high into the Stretford End. "I didn't enjoy, I didn't like, the way they crowded the referee and the penalty spot and tried to affect him,' said Solskjaer. "It clearly worked for them but that's not great to see. But they achieved what they needed to and got what they wanted to. You will be making all these assumptions now on the reaction of players. You know Bruno has been excellent. He is such a good penalty taker and today you'd back him with your mortgage I would guess. That is football. He will step forward every day of the week for this club and this team. Sometimes it just don't go your way. It is such a fine line between Heaven and Hell and unfortunately today he missed. That is going to be the headline isn't it! (Ronaldo v Fernandes). Bruno has been excellent and Cristiano is probably the one that has scored the most penalties in world football. We have got great takers here and it is just a missed opportunity for us to get a point."

Solskjaer made it clear the decision who took the penalty was made before the game and not decided by the players at the time. United had 28 shots yet failed to find the net, the first time Cristiano Ronaldo failed to score since re-signing and the first defeat in the Premier League.

On Match of the Day Alan Shearer agreed with Gary Lineker that Ronaldo would be taking over as the penalty taker, but later Fernandes apologised for his penalty miss and promised fans he will 'be ready next time'.

Former Aston Villa boss Tim Sherwood felt there was "very little" chance of Fernandes taking another penalty with Ronaldo around. "He threw the ball to Ronaldo in an international game and Ronaldo missed one so he's done him a favour there. Listen, he don't miss that. You've never, ever seen him blast the ball over the cross bar. He always waits for the goalkeeper to go down and rolls it in the other corner. Ronaldo [being] there 100% is distorting his thinking there. He knows he's got one chance and one chance only and I think we've just seen it go by."

However, the stats suggested Fernandes was a better penalty taker than Ronaldo! Even with his miss, Fernandes still held a better penalty record at club level, with a 90.7% success rate after converting 39 of 43 club spot-kicks, while Ronaldo had a rate of 85% after scoring 125 from 147 penalties.

Even so, the title race was wide open with a profusion of clubs just a point behind leaders Liverpool. So too was the race for the Golden Boot, with Mo Salah collecting his 100th league goal in the fast time of any Liverpool players with his great mate Croatian centre-half Dejan Lovren referencing Ronaldo on their WhatsApp messages as he asked Salah: "But this year will be interesting, CR7 or MS?"

Solskjaer knew it was now make or break for his management, "We had started the season well until today. It wasn't good enough from us. But I know these players, and I know they will fight to put this right. We have a Champions League game this week and we are looking forward to it. We didn't start well but we will be fired up, the fans and the players, for that.'

It wouldn't be Gary Neville if he wasn't outspoken, and he was sure to have something to say about the current situation with the entire season already on a knife edge. Red Nev's verdict was that this team was an "odd bunch' who 'don't play well enough as a team' to win the title. Plenty of individual quality but there an unclear style of play and little to no cohesion, "I said it even when they were winning, even when Ronaldo scored, they don't play well enough as a team to win this league in my view. They don't play well enough as a team. I think you have to be a unit in and out of possession, and when you only deliver in moments, those moments won't go for you in certain games." Neville wanted to see "patterns of play", and a method of winning when sometimes the team are not performing to their best. "At this moment in time I still see a group of individuals playing in moments, with some patterns and combinations at times, but still a team where some are pretty new together – Cristiano Ronaldo, Raphael Varane, Jadon Sancho – but they've got to come together as a team and start to define a style of play. Then you start to get results when you don't play well. I have called them the odd bunch, because I still look at them and think of them as a team who win games in moments. I look at Chelsea, Liverpool and Man City, they are teams. They put team performances in. That's not to say United never do, but Ole now has to get United into a team."

According to one newspaper report, Ronaldo wanted to continue his association with United by becoming part of the coaching staff. He could end up coaching his son, Cristiano Jr, with the 11-year-old having started training with United's youth teams. Cristiano Jr played for Juventus at youth level scoring four goals on his debut at the age of nine and was being assessed by coaches at United's Littleton Road training complex in Salford.

19: VIVA RONALDO!

*"This is why I came back - I miss this club a lot. I have history
with this club and I want to do it again [win the Champions
League], not only for me but to push the team"*

CRISTIANO RONALDO

Once again 'Viva Ronaldo!' rang out around Old
Trafford as the main man scored an incredible
95th minute winner, ripped off his shirt to show
us all that famous torso of his adoring fans in the Stretford
End, to prove he still has that remarkable six pack and
muscle everywhere you look. This, the latest of late twists,
saw a dramatic goal for United against Villarreal that broke
a club record held by his manager. Ronaldo scored on 94
minutes and 13 seconds at Old Trafford to give United a
2-1 win that not only rescued the tie but rescued their
faltering Champions League campaign and in doing so
he scored United's latest goal in the competition, almost
two minutes deeper into stoppage time than Ole Gunnar
Solskjaer's famous Nou Camp winner which came after 92
minutes and 17 seconds against Bayern Munich.

Whoever writes Ronaldo's scripts should get a pay
rise - what better way to mark his record-breaking 178th
appearance in the Champions League as he overtook
Iker Casillas. The latest United Champions League goal
of all time took Ronaldo's extraordinary record in the

competition to 136 goals in 178 appearances, an astonishing 15 goals ahead of Lionel Messi in the all-time goalscorers' chart who also netted against Manchester City as they beat the English champions 2-0 the previous night.

"This is why I came back - I miss this club a lot. I have history with this club and I want to do it again [win the Champions League], not only for me but to push the team" Ronaldo told reporters after the game. He admitted that United were in a difficult position against Villarreal after their defeat by Young Boys in their opening Champions League tie. "If we did not get the points today, it would be tough to go through to the next stage, but now everything is possible, everything is open and we believe we'll go through."

In truth it had been a hard watch for the United faithful for much of this 'must-win' game, after the shock defeat to Young Boys they faced a team they had never scored a Champions League goal against and who they had just lost to in the Europa League Final the previous May. Villareal may have been without a win in La Liga but they had drawn nearly every other game and this was a difficult game made even harder by a superb performance from the visitors with Danjuma giving stand-in right back Diogo Dalot a torrid time throughout the game. Yet the Spanish side wasted chance after chance and forced David De Gea into a string of fine saves before finally breaking through early in the second half with Danjuma skinning Dalot again to set up Alcacer. United fought back and after Bruno Fernandes fired wide a free kick wide on the right was lofted back towards Alex Telles and the Portuguese left-back fired home a wonderful drive from the edge of the box to level the score. Telles next telling contribution was an incredible goal-line clearance with his back side as Dia seemed certain to win the tie for the Yellow Submarine in the closing stages.

United introduced Cavani, Matic, Fred and Lingard as the hosts searched for a winner and towards the end of the game the visitors understandably tired. Cavani missed a superb chance to win the tie from a superb Greenwood cross but the home side huffed and puffed without really threatening until, in the 95th minute, Fred's cross from the left wing fell for Jesse Lingard close to goal, the England international couldn't get a shot away so touched the ball towards Ronaldo who fired a shot past Villarreal goalkeeper Geronimo Rulli to spark ecstatic celebrations as the goalscorer sprinted off to the corner, whipping off his shirt and throwing it into the air in jubilation as his team-mates and an adoring crowd celebrated wildly.

After the Fergie Time winner the celebrations just went on and on, not just on the field but inside the ground as supporters were still singing 'Viva Ronaldo!' as manager Ole Gunnar Solskjaer was being asked to make sense of the game and outside as fans headed home. It is not hyperbole to say that Cristiano Ronaldo is breathing new life into the Manchester United. He loves the Champions League and is only one winner's medal short of tieing Real Madrid legend Francisco Gento on six and now he has the stage in which to perform his miracle of turning this rag-bag team of stars into a title winning team. They have the talent but can they be moulded into a team? Well, despite the shortcomings, Ronaldo can only help.

Under pressure manager Ole Gunnar Solskjaer has known his fair share of memorable nights at the Theatre of Dreams, but as the fans were sure that they were going to be engulfed in a night of disaster, the manager explained how the emotions, passion and sheer magnetism of the fans helped "suck" the ball into the net!

"That is what happens at Old Trafford, it has happened so many times before. We had to throw caution to the wind and got lucky in the end. Sometimes it is not about 'pass there, pass there', it is the crowd – and they have sucked it in before – and when you have Cristiano on the pitch, you always have a chance. He is so good in front of goal and he has an impact on everyone – the crowd, the players, the whole club.

"He's done that so many times. When you saw him [for Portugal] against Ireland a month ago, he missed a penalty early and didn't touch the ball more or less, but scored two great headers in the last few minutes. That's what he's done throughout his career. He stays in the game. I've seen him all day, the way he's built up for this game and when he gets that one chance it's a goal."

Solskjaer has taken a volume of criticism about the effectiveness of his tactics, especially his substitutions, yet the introduction of Edinson Cavani and Nemanja Matic on 75 minutes and Fred and Lingard 10 minutes later had the desired effect. Owen Hargreaves praised Solskjaer's substitutions saying they provided fresh energy, "when you have players like Cristiano Ronaldo and Cavani who came on and really affected the game, Jesse Lingard as well, Ole got his subs right, he brought on players that could affect the game, they pushed forward, the energy was there, the crowd was up for it, and Cristiano rises to the occasion." Fellow pundit Michael Owen agreed but felt Solskjaer could have benefitted from bringing on Lingard earlier, "The changes certainly worked for Ole, the subs brought so much energy to the game. Cavani, Jesse Lingard, I was surprised Lingard wasn't the first substitute if I'm honest." Owen believed Cavani and Lingard were key to victory compared to Solskjaer's changes against Young Boys. "It's not necessarily about tactics, sometimes it's just about pressure, it's about running, getting people off their seats, dragging your teammates with you," he added. "You've got the energy, the impetus when you come on. You've got to lift the game, make something happen, and I thought Cavani did that and Jesse Lingard at the end was the icing on the cake."

Solskjaer had come under pressure following a humiliating loss in the opening group game against Young Boys and came into this contest following back-to-back home defeats in anything but impressive displays against West Ham and Aston Villa with his team selections and tactics in sharp focus and under constant attack by pundits.

Ronaldo, though, is more often than not a one man match-winner and his fifth goal since his return in Fergie Time, was applauded by none other then than the man who invented United's last gasp winners, Fergie himself, smiling broadly in the stands. The fans stayed inside the stadium long after full-time with their continuous rendition of "Viva Ronaldo", which has become a theme tune for United's season but is clearly a tune that will linger as the No 1 song for this entire Premier League and indeed Europe, as it will be heard everywhere United perform.

"That's some atmosphere," Clinton Morrison told Radio 5 live listeners as he admitted he was "just soaking it in". He added, "when his team needs him, Cristiano Ronaldo produces. Credit to Manchester United - they didn't play that well, but well done to Ronaldo. He can have a quiet night, but that's what world-class players do – they finish like that."

Solskjaer fully agreed when he made the points that "he has done that so many times". It is a constant throughout Ronaldo's career. "He is so strong mentally, he stays in the game and I have seen him all day today, how focused he has been. When he gets that one chance, it is a goal. A true mark of a very good finisher is keeping calm when the chance arrives," a statement backed up by the fact that no player has scored more 90th minute winning goals in Champions League history than Cristiano Ronaldo (he has scored three and is level with Sergio Agüero).

Rio Ferdinand said Ronaldo had texted him to let him know that he always felt as though he was going to score. Speaking to BT Sport after the game, the former United centre-back revealed what Ronaldo messaged him after the game, "He text me tonight saying 'I didn't play well but I knew I'd score'," Ferdinand said, "that's the belief he has. The other players are feeding off it. It's a great place to be. United's performance today wasn't great, it wasn't at the level Ole wants it to be. But when you need a goal, a moment to galvanise the squad, the stadium, the fanbase, Cristiano Ronaldo steps up. He wants to be that guy the chance falls to. His goal record says it all. He's there for the big moments. He's a big part of that too. When you have a player like Cristiano Ronaldo, the players in the dressing room are given life. There's a lease of life, belief, because they know if the chance comes, he will put them away. It gives you that ability to be relaxed. It was the biggest thing in our team. When you get under even more pressure and you can see the clock ticking, you don't panic. We were very composed because we believed the chances would come."

Ronaldo's 2008 Champions League winning team-mate Owen Hargreaves talked about the emotion on the face of Solskjaer as the "stadium went nuts", and that's what Ronaldo gives you, he give you hope "because he can score these big goals" Hargreaves added: "You don't take Ronaldo off because that's what he can do. The stadium got up for them and their big players got them over the line." Michael Owen felt United still relied a bit too much on "individual brilliance", like the goal from Telles, "one of the great goals Old Trafford has seen in the last few years", which pundits likened to one of Paul Scholes greatest ever strikes. Hargreaves, though, had a far more positive observation when he stressed that in the last 10 minutes "it felt more like a team", as there was a huge improvement. He added: "And when you've got Ronaldo, you're always in with a chance of something happening."

Olympic legend Usain Bolt immediately sought out Sir Alex Ferguson after the game to thank him for helping bring back Ronaldo to the club. Speaking to the Manchester Evening News following the match, Bolt said, "He [Ronaldo] helped to build the club and it was wonderful when he was here, the energy. So I'm happy he's back. I just saw Alex Ferguson inside and I thanked him for bringing Cristiano back, so I'm happy about it." The self-confessed fan added, "I'm happy to be here, I haven't been back to Old Trafford in a while, so I'm just happy to be here in the stands with everybody to watch the game."

United faced a tough schedule before the end of November with games against Liverpool, Tottenham, Manchester City, Chelsea and Arsenal in the Premier League and two Champions League meetings with

Atalanta before the return match against Villarreal. It is a month that looked likely to shape their season yet while Solskjaer was on a roller coaster between heaven and hell as he put it, there was only one man with a saintly halo… Viva Ronaldo.

20: WHO IS UNITED'S GREATEST NO.7?

GORDON HILL

Gordon Hill first met Cristiano Ronaldo when he was a kid at United and was struck by how grounded he was. The former United winger who was a fulcrum of Tommy Docherty's fabulous attacking team of the mid seventies is now based in the USA and told me "I met him a few times at Carrington and at Mottram Hall. At first you would have thought he was one of the boys, and as it happened he was. Very confident and knew what he wanted type of guy. Very pleasant and not a 'look at me' type. His ability was there to be seen, and as we have seen he proved he could play at the top and be a top player. We have seen top players look after themselves but to me at his age, has broken all the moulds.

"Would he stand out with the American superstars, I think he would have surpassed them as he has got the personality that would thrive over here. His lifestyle and appearance they would eat it up here. The nice thing about Cristiano is he is down to earth. I have met and sat with the best and he is right at the top. I did not actually talk to him at length basically it was 'Hello how are you doing, and wish you the best and good luck', as a former player would say to a young player as he was still finding his way but I would have thought that Alex was pleased he got such a wonderful talent so young."

Gordon graced the number 11 shirt during his time at United as he and Steve Coppell, who wore no. 7, terrorised defences up and down the land during a fantastic and frenetic 3 year spell at the club which saw him become a huge fan favourite. As for comparisons on the various number 7s who have played for United, Gordon said, " It's difficult because they are all great players and all have special qualities. So wearing the number 7 throws up different players. Bryan Robson for his never say die attitude, Cantona was more a architectural player, Beckham a specialist. Ronaldo is an out-and-out goalscorer. So they all come with great assets. All in the number 7 shirt with special talents and George Best had them all. George was special.

"Bryan Robson would be my first choice from a player's perspective for what he did overall within the team but ranking them to me is what role they play in the team. That's who I would have in a team in midfield and Ronaldo would be more of a forward to me as would Best. Two types of number 7. Midfield number 7 and a forward number 7. All great players but they played different roles That is why ranking them to me is what role they play in the team, looking at it from a former players stand point if you look at his overall performance for his country as well, then yes of course Ronaldo with Robson and George, with Cantona and Beckham next.

1. Ronaldo; 2. Robson; 3. Best; 4. Cantona; 5. Beckham

WES BROWN

Wes was born too late to see much of George Best but is sure many would pick the Irishman as United's greatest ever No 7. But he saw enough of Eric Cantona as a YTS boy at the club to appreciate the Frenchman's impact and of course he shared a dressing room with both Cristiano Ronaldo and David Beckham as a team-mate so in a position to compare all five. "There will be plenty in the United faithful who saw enough of 'Robbo' to put Bryan Robson as the club's greatest No 7" he says.

Wes interviewed Cristiano for MUTV when he returned to Untied.. "Yes I had a little chat with him", Wes says recalling his interview, "it's clear he wants to get on with winning again, and when it comes from someone like him, who has won everything there is to win, you believe him. You only have to look at his stats, his incredible goalscoring record and what he has achieved to see how he wanted to become the best ever and did exactly that and has rejoined United still the best ever. It's the winning mentality, and from what I hear from within the dressing room he has done exactly that, he has brought that winning mentality to everyone around the place."

Wes was sorely tempted to pick Cantona as the club's greatest ever No. 7. "Yes Cantona, for the awe he brought to the club, and what he did was so special. But I have played with Cristiano and watched him close up and the best way to describe him is someone driven to want to learn the game so quickly and to know what needs to be done to reach the top as he did, so it is very hard not say he would be my number one choice, especially when you look at his stats, he is on a different level to just about everyone.

"Then again so many would look at the way 'Robbo' started it all, he was the first to bring that winning mentality to the dressing room, although I must confess I didn't watch that many games when I was young so I didn't that much of him."

So Wes, I am going to put you on the spot. Is it Cantona or Cristiano? Time to make up your mind.

"Ok, here's my choice, and it pains me to put Becks last, but then again it just goes to show the standard of this category, a rich vein of no 7s to have graced the club....

1. Ronaldo; 2. Cantona; 3. Best; 4. Robson; 5. Beckham

BRYAN ROBSON

Who better to discuss the merits of Manchester United's' greatest No 7s than one of the greatest 7s himself, United and England's Captain Marvel? So, putting the question to the current United Ambassador, he rattled off Best, Ronaldo, Beckham and Cantona as the "real stand out ones" but he had another suggestion, "There is one that never gets mentioned, and when I first came to United I played alongside him for the club and for England. In fact I asked Steve for the No 7 shirt and he was happy for me to have it and he played No 11: Steve Coppell. He was a fantastic player, and it was such a shame he had such a bad knee injury. I would certainly put him right up there with the best ever No 7s the club has ever had."

Of course there is one other – Bryan Robson! "It's not easy to talk about yourself!" he admits but plenty of others have as 'Robbo' is in good company with any of the greatest No 7s in the club's history. It might not be easy to talk about his own remarkable and inspirational Captain Fantastic exploits, but he puts Ronaldo first, Best second and while juggling, on the fence, trying to separate Cantona and Best in joint third, he is tempted to put himself third!

Then Beckham and finally Cantona. It's a big surprise that Cantona come last out fo this elite list.

Robbo explains why Beckham just edged out Cantona, "Eric was brilliant in the last four of his five years in English football, maybe the last five of six, but he didn't achieve anything with France, like he did with United but when you look at Becks he won everything there was to win at United but he also had such a wonderful career with England. Eric was amazing for United, the only time the club didn't win the title during those phenomenal years was the season that Eric was banned. Of course you don't want to be praising yourself, but I would be happy enough to be placed behind Ronaldo and Best for sure."

'Robbo' explains why Ronaldo is his No 1 No 7, "for his obvious ability and what he has achieved, it's indisputable that he is the best. People have talked about his age since he came back to United but his fitness levels are still fantastic and he is still producing great football because of that. I am sure he is going to be another 'Giggsie' and play on until he is 40 simply because his fitness levels are so high. As for his return to Old Trafford, he brings back that charisma that has been synonymous with Manchester United and maybe lacking in the recent past.

"The most important thing is the influence he can have over young players, especially forwards like Greenwood, Rashford and Martial – they can see the way he trains, see the way he looks after himself, see his dedication, see the way he still enjoys his training, enjoys his football, always a smile on his around the training ground. If young boys don't look at that and don't take that on board they are never going to be top players, they need to appreciate they are seeing such professionalism and that is the reason you get to the top.

"When I was a young player at West Brom I had players in my position, senior players I looked up to such as Len Cantello and Asa Harford, great midfield players, plus captain John Wyle, they were a big influence on me when I was eleven. The biggest influence would have been watching the World Cup in the house with mum and dad, watching Bobby Moore and Sir Bobby Charlton, they were the great influences in me for sure."

1. Ronaldo; 2. Best; 3. Robson; 4. Beckham; 5. Cantona;
6. Coppell

APPENDIX I - HONOURS

SPORTING

Supertaça Cândido de Oliveira: 2002

MANCHESTER UNITED

Premier League: 2006–07, 2007–08, 2008–09
FA Cup: 2003–04
Football League Cup: 2005–06, 2008–09
FA Community Shield: 2007
UEFA Champions League: 2007–08
FIFA Club World Cup: 2008

REAL MADRID

La Liga: 2011–12, 2016–17
Copa del Rey: 2010–11, 2013–14
Supercopa de España: 2012, 2017
UEFA Champions League: 2013–14, 2015–16, 2016–17,
2017–18
UEFA Super Cup: 2014, 2017
FIFA Club World Cup: 2014, 2016, 2017

JUVENTUS

Serie A: 2018–19, 2019–20
Coppa Italia: 2020–21
Supercoppa Italiana: 2018, 2020

PORTUGAL

UEFA European Championship: 2016
UEFA Nations League: 2018–19

INDIVIDUAL AWARDS

FIFA Ballon d'Or/Ballon d'Or: 2008, 2013, 2014, 2016, 2017
FIFA World Player of the Year: 2008
The Best FIFA Men's Player: 2016, 2017
European Golden Shoe: 2007–08, 2010–11, 2013–14, 2014–15
FPF Portuguese Player of the Year: 2016, 2017, 2018, 2019
PFA Players' Player of the Year: 2006–07, 2007–08
Premier League Player of the Season: 2006–07, 2007–08
Premier League Golden Boot: 2007–08
La Liga Best Player: 2013–14
Pichichi Trophy: 2010–11, 2013–14, 2014–15
Serie A Footballer of the Year: 2019, 2020
Capocannoniere: 2020–21

APPENDIX II - SEASON BY SEASON

MANCHESTER UNITED 2003-2009

2003-04

Date		Opponent					Scorers
16-08-2003	PL	Bolton Wanderers	4	0	H	0	Giggs 35', 74', Scholes 77', van Nistlerooy 87'
23-08-2003	PL	Newcastle United	2	1	A	0	van Nistlerooy 51', Scholes 59'
27-08-2003	PL	Wolves	1	0	H	0	O'Shea 10'
31-08-2003	PL	Southampton	0	1	A	0	
13-09-2003	PL	Charlton Athletic	2	0	A	0	Van Nistlerooy 62' 82'
21-09-2003	PL	Arsenal	0	0	H	0	
01-10-2003	CL	Stuttgart	1	2	A	0	Van Nistlerooy 67' (pen)
18-10-2003	PL	Leeds United	1	0	A	0	Keane 81'
25-10-2003	PL	Fulham	1	3	H	0	Forlan 45'
01-11-2003	PL	Portsmouth	3	0	H	1	Forlan 37', Ronaldo 80', Keane 82'
04-11-2003	CL	Rangers	3	0	H	0	Forlan 6', Van Nistlerooy 43', 60'
22-11-2003	PL	Blackburn Rovers	2	1	A	0	Van Nistlerooy 24', Kleberson 38'
26-11-2003	CL	Panathinaikos	1	0	A	0	Forlan 85'
30-11-2003	PL	Chelsea	0	1	A	0	
03-12-2003	LC	West Bromwich Albion	0	2	A	0	
06-12-2003	PL	Aston Villa	4	0	H	0	Van Nistlerooy 16', 45', Forlan 90', 90'
13-12-2003	PL	Manchester City	3	1	H	0	Scholes 7', 73', Van Nistlerooy 34'
21-12-2003	PL	Tottenham Hotspur	2	1	A	0	O'Shea 15', Van Nistlerooy 26'
26-12-2003	PL	Everton	3	2	H	0	Butt 9', Kleberson 44', Bellion 68'
17-01-2004	PL	Wolves	0	1	A	0	
25-01-2004	FAC	Northampton Town	3	0	A	0	Silvestre 34', Hargreaves 47' (o.g.), Forlan 68'
31-01-2004	PL	Southampton	3	2	H	0	Saha 18', Scholes 37', Van Nistlerooy 61'
07-02-2004	PL	Everton	4	3	A	0	Saha 9', 29', Van Nistlerooy 24', 89'
11-02-2004	PL	Middlesbrough	2	3	H	0	Van Nistlerooy 45', Giggs 63'
14-02-2004	FAC	Manchester City	4	2	H	1	Scholes 34', Van Nistlerooy 71', 80', Ronaldo 74'
25-02-2004	CL	Porto	1	2	A	0	Fortune 14'
28-02-2004	PL	Fulham	1	1	A	0	Saha 14'
06-03-2004	FAC	Fulham	2	1	H	0	Van Nistlerooy 25', 62'
09-03-2004	CL	Porto	1	1	H	0	Scholes 32'
14-03-2004	PL	Manchester City	1	4	A	0	Scholes 35'
20-03-2004	PL	Tottenham Hotspur	3	0	H	1	Giggs 30', Ronaldo 89', Bellion 90'
03-04-2004	FAC	Arsenal	1	0	N	0	Scholes 32'
10-04-2004	PL	Birmingham City	2	1	A	1	Ronaldo 60', Saha 78'
13-04-2004	PL	Leicester City	1	0	H	0	Gary Neville 56'
17-04-2004	PL	Portsmouth	0	1	A	0	
20-04-2004	PL	Charlton Athletic	2	0	H	0	Saha 28', Gary Neville 65'
24-04-2004	PL	Liverpool	0	1	H	0	
08-05-2004	PL	Chelsea	1	1	H	0	Van Nistlerooy 76'
15-05-2004	PL	Aston Villa	2	0	A	1	Ronaldo 4', Van Nistlerooy 10'

| 22-05-2004 | FAC | Millwall | 3 | 0 | N | 1 | Ronaldo 44', Van Nistlerooy 65' (pen), 81' |

2004-05

21-08-2004	PL	Norwich City	2	1	H	0	Bellion 32', Smith 50'
25-08-2004	CL	Dinamo Bucharest	3	0	H	0	Smith 47', 50', Bellion 70'
28-08-2004	PL	Blackburn Rovers	1	1	A	0	Smith 90'+3
30-08-2004	PL	Everton	0	0	H	0	
11-09-2004	PL	Bolton Wanderers	2	2	A	0	Gabriel Heinze 44', Bellion 90'+2
15-09-2004	CL	Olympique Lyonnais	2	2	A	0	Van Nistlerooy 56', 61'
20-09-2004	PL	Liverpool	2	1	H	0	Silvestre 20', 66'
25-09-2004	PL	Tottenham Hotspur	1	0	A	0	Van Nistlerooy 42' (pen)
03-10-2004	PL	Middlesbrough	1	1	H	0	Smith 81'
16-10-2004	PL	Birmingham City	0	0	A	0	
19-10-2004	CL	Sparta Prague	0	0	A	0	
24-10-2004	PL	Arsenal	2	0	H	0	Van Nistlerooy 73' (pen), Rooney 90'
30-10-2004	PL	Portsmouth	0	2	A	0	
03-11-2004	CL	Sparta Prague	4	1	H	0	Van Nistlerooy 14', 25' (pen), 60', 90'
07-11-2004	PL	Manchester City	0	0	H	0	
14-11-2004	PL	Newcastle United	3	1	A	0	Rooney 7', 90', Van Nistlerooy 74' (pen)
23-11-2004	CL	Olympique Lyonnais	2	1	H	0	Gary Neville 19', Van Nistlerooy 53'
27-11-2004	PL	West Bromwich Albion	3	0	A	0	Scholes 53', 82', Van Nistlerooy 72'
04-12-2004	PL	Southampton	3	0	H	1	Scholes 53', Rooney 58', Ronaldo 87'
08-12-2004	CL	Fenerbahce	0	3	A	0	
13-12-2004	PL	Fulham	1	1	A	0	Smith 33'
26-12-2004	PL	Bolton Wanderers	2	0	H	0	Giggs 10', Scholes 89'
28-12-2004	PL	Aston Villa	1	0	A	0	Giggs 41'
01-01-2005	PL	Middlesbrough	2	0	A	0	Fletcher 9', Giggs 79'
04-01-2005	PL	Tottenham Hotspur	0	0	H	0	
08-01-2005	FAC	Exeter City	0	0	H	0	
12-01-2005	LC	Chelsea	0	0	A	0	
15-01-2005	PL	Liverpool	1	0	A	0	Rooney 21'
19-01-2005	FAC	Exeter City	2	0	A	1	Ronaldo 9', Rooney 87'
22-01-2005	PL	Aston Villa	3	1	H	1	Ronaldo 8', Saha 69', Scholes 70'
26-01-2005	LC	Chelsea	1	2	H	0	Giggs 67'
29-01-2005	FAC	Middlesbrough	3	0	H	0	O'Shea 10', Rooney 67', 82'
01-02-2005	PL	Arsenal	4	2	A	2	Cole (o.g.) 18', Ronaldo 54', 58', O'Shea 89'
05-02-2005	PL	Birmingham City	2	0	H	0	Keane 55', Rooney 78'
13-02-2005	PL	Manchester City	2	0	A	0	Rooney 68', Richard Dunne 75' (o.g.)
19-02-2005	FAC	Everton	2	0	A	1	Fortune 23', Ronaldo 58'
23-02-2005	CL	AC Milan	0	1	H	0	
26-02-2005	PL	Portsmouth	2	1	H	0	Rooney 8', 81'
05-03-2005	PL	Crystal Palace	0	0	A	0	
08-03-2005	CL	AC Milan	0	1	A	0	
12-03-2005	FAC	Southampton	4	0	A	1	Keane 2', Ronaldo 45', Scholes 48', 87'
19-03-2005	PL	Fulham	1	0	H	1	Ronaldo 21'
02-04-2005	PL	Blackburn Rovers	0	0	H	0	

09-04-2005	PL	Norwich City	0	2	A	0	
17-04-2005	FAC	Newcastle United	4	1	N	1	Van Nistlerooy 19', 58', Scholes 45', Ronaldo 76'
20-04-2005	PL	Everton	0	1	A	0	
24-04-2005	PL	Newcastle United	2	1	H	0	Rooney 57', Wesley Brown 75'
07-05-2005	PL	West Bromwich Albion	1	1	H	0	Giggs 21'
10-05-2005	PL	Chelsea	1	3	H	0	Van Nistlerooy 7'
21-05-2005	FAC	Arsenal	0	0	N	0	

2005-06

09-08-2005	CL	Debreceni Vsc	3	0	H	1	Rooney 7', Van Nistlerooy 49', Ronaldo 63'
20-08-2005	PL	Aston Villa	1	0	H	0	Van Nistlerooy 66'
24-08-2005	CL	Debreceni Vsc	3	0	A	0	Gabriel Heinze 20', 61', Richardson 65'
28-08-2005	PL	Newcastle United	2	0	A	0	Rooney 66', Van Nistlerooy 90'
14-09-2005	CL	Villarreal	0	0	A	0	
18-09-2005	PL	Liverpool	0	0	A	0	
24-09-2005	PL	Blackburn Rovers	1	2	H	0	Van Nistlerooy 67'
27-09-2005	CL	Benfica	2	1	H	0	Giggs 39', Van Nistlerooy 85'
01-10-2005	PL	Fulham	3	2	A	0	Van Nistlerooy 16' (pen), 44', Rooney 17'
15-10-2005	PL	Sunderland	3	1	A	0	Rooney 40', Van Nistlerooy 76', Rossi 87'
18-10-2005	CL	Lille	0	0	H	0	
22-10-2005	PL	Tottenham Hotspur	1	1	H	0	Silvestre 7'
29-10-2005	PL	Middlesbrough	1	4	H	1	Ronaldo 90'
02-11-2005	CL	Lille	0	1	A	0	
06-11-2005	PL	Chelsea	1	0	H	0	Fletcher 31'
19-11-2005	PL	Charlton Athletic	3	1	A	0	Smith 37', Van Nistlerooy 70', 85'
22-11-2005	CL	Villarreal	0	0	H	0	
30-11-2005	LC	West Bromwich Albion	3	1	H	1	Ronaldo 12' (pen), Saha 16', O'Shea 56'
03-12-2005	PL	Portsmouth	3	0	H	0	Scholes 20', Rooney 80', Van Nistlerooy 84'
07-12-2005	CL	Benfica	1	2	A	0	Scholes 6'
11-12-2005	PL	Everton	1	1	H	0	Giggs 15'
14-12-2005	PL	Wigan Athletic	4	0	H	0	Ferdinand 30', Rooney 35', 55', Van Nistlerooy 70' (pen)
17-12-2005	PL	Aston Villa	2	0	A	0	Van Nistlerooy 10', Rooney 51'
20-12-2005	LC	Birmingham City	3	1	A	0	Saha 46', 63', Park 50'
28-12-2005	PL	Birmingham City	2	2	A	0	Van Nistlerooy 4', Rooney 53'
31-12-2005	PL	Bolton Wanderers	4	1	H	2	N'Gotty 8' (o.g.), Saha 44', Ronaldo 68', 90'
03-01-2006	PL	Arsenal	0	0	A	0	
08-01-2006	FAC	Burton Albion	0	0	A	0	
11-01-2006	LC	Blackburn Rovers	1	1	A	0	Saha 30'
14-01-2006	PL	Manchester City	1	3	A	0	Van Nistlerooy 76'
01-02-2006	PL	Blackburn Rovers	3	4	A	0	Saha 37', Van Nistlerooy 63' 65'
04-02-2006	PL	Fulham	4	2	H	2	Bocanegra 6' (o.g.), Ronaldo 14', 86', Saha 23'
11-02-2006	PL	Portsmouth	3	1	A	2	Van Nistlerooy 18', Ronaldo 38', 45'
18-02-2006	FAC	Liverpool	0	1	A	0	
26-02-2006	LC	Wigan Athletic	4	0	N	1	Rooney 33', 61', Saha 55', Ronaldo 59'
06-03-2006	PL	Wigan Athletic	2	1	A	1	Ronaldo 74', Chimbonda 90' (o.g.)
12-03-2006	PL	Newcastle United	2	0	H	0	Rooney 8', 12'

18-03-2006	PL	West Bromwich Albion	2	1	A	0	Saha 16', 64'
26-03-2006	PL	Birmingham City	3	0	H	0	Giggs 3', 15', Rooney 83'
29-03-2006	PL	West Ham United	1	0	H	0	Van Nistlerooy 45'
01-04-2006	PL	Bolton Wanderers	2	1	A	0	Saha 33', Van Nistlerooy 79'
09-04-2006	PL	Arsenal	2	0	H	0	Rooney 54', Park 78'
14-04-2006	PL	Sunderland	0	0	H	0	
17-04-2006	PL	Tottenham Hotspur	2	1	A	0	Rooney 8', 36'
29-04-2006	PL	Chelsea	0	3	A	0	
01-05-2006	PL	Middlesbrough	0	0	H	0	
07-05-2006	PL	Charlton Athletic	4	0	H	1	Saha 19', Ronaldo 23', Euell 34' (o.g.), Richardson 58'

2006-07

20-08-2006	PL	Fulham	5	1	H	1	Saha 8', Pearce 14' (o.g.), Rooney 16', 64', Ronaldo 19'
23-08-2006	PL	Charlton Athletic	3	0	A	0	Fletcher 49', Saha, 80', Solskjaer 90'
26-08-2006	PL	Watford	2	1	A	0	Silvestre 12', Giggs 52'
09-09-2006	PL	Tottenham Hotspur	1	0	H	0	Giggs 9'
17-09-2006	PL	Arsenal	0	1	H	0	
23-09-2006	PL	Reading	1	1	A	1	Ronaldo 73'
26-09-2006	CL	Benfica	1	0	A	0	Saha 60'
01-10-2006	PL	Newcastle United	2	0	H	0	Solskjaer 41', 49'
17-10-2006	CL	Copenhagen	3	0	H	0	Scholes 39', O'Shea 46', Richardson 83'
28-10-2006	PL	Bolton Wanderers	4	0	A	1	Rooney 10', 16', 89', Ronaldo 82'
01-11-2006	CL	Copenhagen	0	1	A	0	
04-11-2006	PL	Portsmouth	3	0	H	1	Saha 3' (pen), Ronaldo 10', Vidic 66'
07-11-2006	LC	Southend United	0	1	A	0	
11-11-2006	PL	Blackburn Rovers	1	0	A	0	Saha 64'
18-11-2006	PL	Sheffield United	2	1	A	0	Rooney 30', 75'
21-11-2006	CL	Celtic	0	1	A	0	
26-11-2006	PL	Chelsea	1	1	H	0	Saha 29'
29-11-2006	PL	Everton	3	0	H	1	Ronaldo 39', Evra 63', O'Shea 88'
02-12-2006	PL	Middlesbrough	2	1	A	0	Saha 19' (pen), Fletcher 68'
06-12-2006	CL	Benfica	3	1	H	0	Vidic 45', Giggs 61', Saha 75'
09-12-2006	PL	Manchester City	3	1	H	1	Rooney 6', Saha 45', Ronaldo 84'
17-12-2006	PL	West Ham United	0	1	A	0	
23-12-2006	PL	Aston Villa	3	0	A	2	Ronaldo 58', 85', Scholes 64'
26-12-2006	PL	Wigan Athletic	3	1	H	2	Ronaldo 47', 51', Solskjaer 59'
30-12-2006	PL	Reading	3	2	H	2	Solskjaer 33', Ronaldo 59', 77'
01-01-2007	PL	Newcastle United	2	2	A	0	Scholes 14', 46'
07-01-2007	FAC	Aston Villa	2	1	H	0	Larsson 55', Solskjaer 90'
13-01-2007	PL	Aston Villa	3	1	H	1	Park 11', Carrick 13', Ronaldo 35'
21-01-2007	PL	Arsenal	1	2	A	0	Rooney 53'
31-01-2007	PL	Watford	4	0	H	1	Ronaldo 20' (pen), Doyley 60' (o.g.), Larsson 70', Rooney 71'
04-02-2007	PL	Tottenham Hotspur	4	0	A	1	Ronaldo 45' (pen), Vidic 48', Scholes 52', Giggs 77'
17-02-2007	FAC	Reading	1	1	H	0	Carrick 45'
20-02-2007	CL	Lille	1	0	A	0	Giggs 83'

24-02-2007	PL	Fulham	2	1	A	1	Giggs 29', Ronaldo 88'
27-02-2007	FAC	Reading	3	2	A	0	Gabriel Heinze 2', Saha 4', Solskjaer 6'
03-03-2007	PL	Liverpool	1	0	A	0	O'Shea 90'+1
07-03-2007	CL	Lille	1	0	H	0	Larsson 72'
10-03-2007	FAC	Middlesbrough	2	2	A	1	Rooney 23', Ronaldo 68' (pen)
17-03-2007	PL	Bolton Wanderers	4	1	H	0	Park 14', 25', Rooney 17', 74'
19-03-2007	FAC	Middlesbrough	1	0	H	1	Ronaldo 76' (pen)
31-03-2007	PL	Blackburn Rovers	4	1	H	0	Scholes 61', Carrick 72', Park 83', Solskjaer 90'
04-04-2007	CL	Roma	1	2	A	0	Rooney 60'
07-04-2007	PL	Portsmouth	1	2	A	0	O'Shea 90'
10-04-2007	CL	Roma	7	1	H	2	Carrick 11', 60', Smith 17', Rooney 18', Ronaldo 44', 49', Evra 81'
14-04-2007	FAC	Watford	4	1	N	1	Rooney 7', 66', Ronaldo 28', Richardson 82'
17-04-2007	PL	Sheffield United	2	0	H	0	Carrick 4', Rooney 50'
21-04-2007	PL	Middlesbrough	1	1	H	0	Richardson 3'
24-04-2007	CL	AC Milan	3	2	H	1	Ronaldo 5', Rooney 59', 90'
28-04-2007	PL	Everton	4	2	A	0	O'Shea 61', Neville 68' (o.g.), Rooney 79', Eagles 90'
02-05-2007	CL	AC Milan	0	3	A	0	
05-05-2007	PL	Manchester City	1	0	A	1	Ronaldo 34' (pen)
13-05-2007	PL	West Ham United	0	1	H	0	
19-05-2007	FAC	Chelsea	0	1	N	0	

2007-08

05-08-2007	CS	Chelsea	1	1	N	0	Giggs 35'
12-08-2007	PL	Reading	0	0	H	0	
15-08-2007	PL	Portsmouth	1	1	A	0	Scholes 15'
15-09-2007	PL	Everton	1	0	A	0	Vidic 83'
19-09-2007	CL	Sporting Club Lisbon	1	0	A	1	Ronaldo 72'
23-09-2007	PL	Chelsea	2	0	H	0	Tevez 45', Saha 89' (pen)
29-09-2007	PL	Birmingham City	1	0	A	1	Ronaldo 52'
02-10-2007	CL	Roma	1	0	H	0	Rooney 70'
06-10-2007	PL	Wigan Athletic	4	0	H	2	Tevez 54', Ronaldo 59', 76', Rooney 82'
20-10-2007	PL	Aston Villa	4	1	A	0	Rooney 36', 44', Ferdinand 45', Giggs 75'
23-10-2007	CL	Dynamo Kiev	4	2	A	2	Ferdinand 10', Rooney 18', Ronaldo 41', 68' (pen)
27-10-2007	PL	Middlesbrough	4	1	H	0	Nani 3', Rooney 33', Tevez 55', 85'
03-11-2007	PL	Arsenal	2	2	A	1	Gallas 45' (o.g.), Ronaldo 82'
07-11-2007	CL	Dynamo Kiev	4	0	H	1	Pique 31', Tevez 37', Rooney 76', Ronaldo 88'
11-11-2007	PL	Blackburn Rovers	2	0	H	2	Ronaldo 34', 35'
27-11-2007	CL	Sporting Club Lisbon	2	1	H	1	Tevez 61', Ronaldo 90'
03-12-2007	PL	Fulham	2	0	H	2	Ronaldo 10', 58'
08-12-2007	PL	Derby County	4	1	H	1	Giggs 40', Tevez 45', 60', Ronaldo 90'
16-12-2007	PL	Liverpool	1	0	A	0	Tevez 43'
23-12-2007	PL	Everton	2	1	H	2	Ronaldo 22', 88' (pen)
26-12-2007	PL	Sunderland	4	0	H	1	Rooney 20', Saha 30', 86' (pen), Ronaldo 45'
29-12-2007	PL	West Ham United	1	2	A	1	Ronaldo 14'
01-01-2008	PL	Birmingham City	1	0	H	0	Tevez 25'
05-01-2008	FAC	Aston Villa	2	0	A	1	Ronaldo 81', Rooney 89'

12-01-2008	PL	Newcastle United	6	0	H	3	Ronaldo 49', 70', 88', Tevez 55', 90', Rio Ferdinand 85'
19-01-2008	PL	Reading	2	0	A	1	Rooney 77', Ronaldo 90'
27-01-2008	FAC	Tottenham Hotspur	3	1	H	2	Tevez 38', Ronaldo 69' (pen), 88'
30-01-2008	PL	Portsmouth	2	0	H	2	Ronaldo 10', 13'
02-02-2008	PL	Tottenham Hotspur	1	1	A	0	Tevez 90'
10-02-2008	PL	Manchester City	1	2	H	0	Carrick 90'
20-02-2008	CL	Olympique Lyonnais	1	1	A	0	Tevez 87'
23-02-2008	PL	Newcastle United	5	1	A	2	Rooney 25', 80', Ronaldo 45', 56', Saha 90'
01-03-2008	PL	Fulham	3	0	A	0	Owen Hargreaves 15', Park 44', Davies 72' (o.g.)
04-03-2008	CL	Olympique Lyonnais	1	0	H	1	Ronaldo 41'
08-03-2008	FAC	Portsmouth	0	1	H	0	
15-03-2008	PL	Derby County	1	0	A	1	Ronaldo 76'
19-03-2008	PL	Bolton Wanderers	2	0	H	2	Ronaldo 9', 20'
23-03-2008	PL	Liverpool	3	0	H	1	Brown 34', Ronaldo 79', Nani 81'
29-03-2008	PL	Aston Villa	4	0	H	1	Ronaldo 17', Tevez 33', Rooney 53', 70'
01-04-2008	CL	Roma	2	0	A	1	Ronaldo 39', Rooney 66'
06-04-2008	PL	Middlesbrough	2	2	A	1	Ronaldo 10', Rooney 74'
13-04-2008	PL	Arsenal	2	1	H	1	Ronaldo 54' (pen), Hargreaves 72'
19-04-2008	PL	Blackburn Rovers	1	1	A	0	Tevez 88'
23-04-2008	CL	Barcelona	0	0	A	0	
26-04-2008	PL	Chelsea	1	2	A	0	Rooney 56'
29-04-2008	CL	Barcelona	1	0	H	0	Scholes 14'
03-05-2008	PL	West Ham United	4	1	H	2	Ronaldo 3', 24', Tevez 26', Carrick 59'
11-05-2008	PL	Wigan Athletic	2	0	A	1	Ronaldo 33' (pen), Giggs 80'
21-05-2008	CL	Chelsea	1	1	N	1	Ronaldo 26'

2008-09

17-09-2008	CL	Villarreal	0	0	H	0	
21-09-2008	PL	Chelsea	1	1	A	0	Park 18'
23-09-2008	LC	Middlesbrough	3	1	H	1	Ronaldo 25', Giggs 79', Nani 90'
27-09-2008	PL	Bolton Wanderers	2	0	H	1	Ronaldo 60' (pen), Rooney 77'
30-09-2008	CL	Aa Aalborg	3	0	A	0	Rooney 22', Berbatov 55', 79'
04-10-2008	PL	Blackburn Rovers	2	0	A	0	Wesley Brown 31', Rooney 64'
18-10-2008	PL	West Bromwich Albion	4	0	H	1	Rooney 56', Ronaldo 69', Berbatov 72', Nani 90'
21-10-2008	CL	Celtic	3	0	H	0	Berbatov 30', 51', Rooney 76'
25-10-2008	PL	Everton	1	1	A	0	Fletcher 21'
29-10-2008	PL	West Ham United	2	0	H	2	Ronaldo 14', 30'
01-11-2008	PL	Hull City	4	3	H	2	Ronaldo 3', 44', Carrick 29', Vidic 57'
05-11-2008	CL	Celtic	1	1	A	0	Giggs 85'
08-11-2008	PL	Arsenal	1	2	A	0	Rafael da Silva 90'
15-11-2008	PL	Stoke City	5	0	H	2	Ronaldo 3', 89', Carrick 45', Berbatov 49', Welbeck 84'
22-11-2008	PL	Aston Villa	0	0	A	0	
25-11-2008	CL	Villarreal	0	0	A	0	
30-11-2008	PL	Manchester City	1	0	A	0	Rooney 42'
06-12-2008	PL	Sunderland	1	0	H	0	Vidic 90'
13-12-2008	PL	Tottenham Hotspur	0	0	A	0	

18-12-2008	CWC	Gamba Osaka	5 3 N	1	Vidic 28', Ronaldo 45', Rooney 75', 80', Fletcher 77'
21-12-2008	CWC	Ldu Quito	1 0 N	0	Rooney 73'
26-12-2008	PL	Stoke City	1 0 A	0	Tevez 83'
29-12-2008	PL	Middlesbrough	1 0 H	0	Berbatov 69'
07-01-2009	LC	Derby County	0 1 A	0	
11-01-2009	PL	Chelsea	3 0 H	0	Vidic 45', Rooney 63', Berbatov 87'
14-01-2009	PL	Wigan Athletic	1 0 H	0	Rooney 1'
17-01-2009	PL	Bolton Wanderers	1 0 A	0	Berbatov 90'
20-01-2009	LC	Derby County	4 2 H	1	Nani 16', O'Shea 22', Tevez 34', Ronaldo 89' (pen)
24-01-2009	FAC	Tottenham Hotspur	2 1 H	0	Scholes 35', Berbatov 36'
27-01-2009	PL	West Bromwich Albion	5 0 A	2	Berbatov 22', Tevez 44', Vidic 60', Ronaldo 65', 73'
31-01-2009	PL	Everton	1 0 H	1	Ronaldo 44' (pen)
08-02-2009	PL	West Ham United	1 0 A	0	Giggs 62'
15-02-2009	FAC	Derby County	4 1 A	1	Nani 29', Gibson 44', Ronaldo 48', Welbeck 81'
18-02-2009	PL	Fulham	3 0 H	0	Scholes 12', Berbatov 30', Rooney 63'
21-02-2009	PL	Blackburn Rovers	2 1 H	1	Rooney 23', Ronaldo 60'
24-02-2009	CL	Inter Milan	0 0 A	0	
01-03-2009	LC	Tottenham Hotspur	0 0 N	0	
04-03-2009	PL	Newcastle United	2 1 A	0	Rooney 20', Berbatov 56'
11-03-2009	CL	Inter Milan	2 0 H	1	Vidic 4', Ronaldo 49'
14-03-0000	PL	Liverpool	1 4 H	1	Ronaldo 23' (pen)
21-03-2009	PL	Fulham	0 2 A	0	
05-04-2009	PL	Aston Villa	3 2 H	2	Ronaldo 13', 81', Macheda 90'
07-04-2009	CL	Porto	2 2 H	0	Rooney 15', Tevez 86'
11-04-2009	PL	Sunderland	2 1 A	0	Scholes 19', Macheda 75'
15-04-2009	CL	Porto	1 0 A	1	Ronaldo 5'
22-04-2009	PL	Portsmouth	2 0 H	0	Rooney 9', Carrick 82'
25-04-2009	PL	Tottenham Hotspur	5 2 H	2	Ronaldo 57' (pen), 68', Rooney 67', 71', Berbatov 79'
29-04-2009	CL	Arsenal	1 0 H	0	O'Shea 17'
05-05-2009	CL	Arsenal	3 1 A	2	Park 8', Ronaldo 11', 61'
10-05-2009	PL	Manchester City	2 0 H	1	Ronaldo 18', Tevez 45'
13-05-2009	PL	Wigan Athletic	2 1 A	0	Tevez 61', Carrick 86'
16-05-2009	PL	Arsenal	0 0 H	0	
27-05-2009	CL	Barcelona	0 2 N	0	

SUMMARY - MANCHESTER UNITED 2003-09

	PL		LC		FAC		CS		CL		CWC		TOTAL	
	GL	GM	GL	GM	GL	GM	GL	GM	GL	GM	GL	GM	GL	GM
2003-2004	4	29	0	1	2	5	0	0	0	5	0	0	6	40
2004-2005	5	33	0	2	4	7	0	0	0	8	0	0	9	50
2005-2006	9	33	2	4	0	2	0	0	1	8	0	0	12	47
2006-2007	17	34	0	1	3	7	0	0	3	11	0	0	23	53
2007-2008	31	34	0	0	3	3	0	1	8	11	0	0	42	49
2008-2009	18	33	2	4	1	2	0	0	4	12	1	2	26	53

REAL MADRID 2009-18

	LEAGUE		CUP		CL		OTHER		TOTAL	
	GMS	GLS	GMS	GLS	GMS	GLS	GMS	GLS	GMS	GLS
2009-10	29	26	0	0	6	7	–	–	35	33
2010-11	34	40[g]	8	7	12	6	–	–	54	53
2011-12	38	46	5	3	10	10	2[h]	1	55	60
2012-13	34	34	7	7	12	12	2[h]	2	55	55
2013-14	30	31	6	3	11	17	–	–	47	51
2014-15	35	48	2	1	12	10	5[i]	2	54	61
2015-16	36	35	0	0	12	16	–	–	48	51
2016-17	29	25	2	1	13	12	2[f]	4	46	42
2017-18	27	26	0	0	13	15	4[j]	3	44	44
TOTAL	292	311	30	22	–	105	15	12	438	450

JUVENTUS 2018-21

	LEAGUE		CUP		CL		OTHER		TOTAL	
	GMS	GLS	GMS	GLS	GMS	GLS	GMS	GLS	GMS	GLS
2018-19	31	21	2	0	9	6	1[k]	1	43	28
2019-20	33	31	4	2	8	4	1[k]	0	46	37
2020-21	33	29	4	2	6	4	1[k]	1	44	36
2021-22	1	0	0	0	0	0	0	0	1	0
TOTAL	98	81	10	4	23	14	3	2	134	101

PORTUGAL 2003-21

	GAMES	GOALS		GAMES	GOALS
2003	2	0	2013	9	10
2004	16	7	2014	9	5
2005	11	2	2015	5	3
2006	14	6	2016	13	13
2007	10	5	2017	11	11
2008	8	1	2018	7	6
2009	7	1	2019	10	14
2010	11	3	2020	6	3
2011	8	7	2021	10	9
2012	13	5	Total	180	111

Printed in Great Britain
by Amazon